G. K Woods

Personal Impressions of the Grand Cañon of the Colorado River

Near Flagstaff, Arizona

G. K Woods

Personal Impressions of the Grand Cañon of the Colorado River
Near Flagstaff, Arizona

ISBN/EAN: 9783337205577

Printed in Europe, USA, Canada, Australia, Japan

Cover: Foto ©Andreas Hilbeck / pixelio.de

More available books at **www.hansebooks.com**

CAPTAIN JOHN HANCE,
The well-known Guide of the Grand Cañon of the Colorado River.

PERSONAL IMPRESSIONS

OF THE

Grand Cañon of the Colorado River

NEAR FLAGSTAFF, ARIZONA

AS SEEN THROUGH NEARLY TWO THOUSAND EYES, AND
WRITTEN IN THE PRIVATE VISITORS' BOOK
OF THE WORLD-FAMOUS GUIDE

CAPT. JOHN HANCE

GUIDE, STORY-TELLER, AND PATH-FINDER

COLLECTED AND COMPILED BY

G. K. WOODS

PUBLISHED FOR G. K. WOODS, FLAGSTAFF, ARIZONA TERRITORY

BY

THE WHITAKER & RAY COMPANY
SAN FRANCISCO

1899

Copyright, 1899, by
G. K. WOODS.

DEDICATION

TO THE PATRONS OF THIS WORK

THIS work is respectfully dedicated the many writers who have enabled me to present to the world ideas of what this great masterpiece of nature looks like (by their gratuitous contributions of the impression made upon their minds after viewing this stupendous cañon), and I sincerely hope that the many tourists, pleasure-seekers, and students of nature who in the future visit this grand work of nature will bestow on those who have herein contributed to the enlightenment of the people at large full measure for their expressions.

Respectfully yours,

G. K. WOODS.

J. WILBUR THURBER,
The efficient Proprietor of the Stage Line from Flagstaff to the Grand Cañon.

PREFACE.

To the Patrons of this Volume: This is not a descriptive writing on the Grand Cañon of the Colorado River, but a record of the impressions created upon the minds of individual visitors, at various times and under different circumstances, and written in the private visitors' book of Capt. John Hance, the famous Grand Cañon guide. It covers a period of ten years, and partially describes the trip by stage from Flagstaff, Arizona, and return, under the management of G. K. Woods, General Manager of the Grand Cañon stage line, owned and operated by J. Wilbur Thurbur.

G. K. WOODS.

Flagstaff, A. T., March 1, 1899.

CONTENTS.

	PAGE
Flagstaff, Arizona	15
To the Traveling Public	19
The Grand Cañon of the Colorado River (by J. Curtis Wasson)	23
Notice to the Reader	29
Personal Impressions of the Grand Cañon of the Colorado River	31
Poem: The Grand Cañon of the Colorado (by C. R. Pattee)	129
The Stalactite Caves of the Grand Cañon (by J. Curtis Wasson)	133
"The World Is Cleft" — ("Fitz-Mac" on the Wonders of the Grand Cañon)	137
The Grand Cañon Cavern	149
An Enthusiastic Description (by G. Wharton James)	155
The Grand Cañon	161
How to Get There	163

ILLUSTRATIONS.

	PAGE
Frontispiece (Capt. John Hance)	
J. Wilbur Thurbur	6
Flagstaff, Arizona	14
G. K. Woods	18
Colorado River — Foot of Grand View Trail	22
Grandeur Ridge — on the Grand View Trail	28
San Francisco Mountains	35
Cottonwood Cañon	41
Horseshoe Point — Grand View Trail	47
Mode of Travel in the Grand Cañon	53
Scene on the Grand View Trail	58
Colorado River — Looking up from Grand View Trail	67
Water Train — Grand View Trail	75
A Resting-Place — Head of Grand View Trail	83
A Commodious Tent — Grand Cañon	91
Chimney Rock — Grand Cañon	99
Scene from Hotel Point — Grand Cañon	107
Waterfall — Grand Cañon	115
Original Hance Cabin, 1885	123
Head of Cottonwood Cañon — Grand View Trail	128
Scene in the Stalactite Caves	132
Hance Falls — Grand Cañon	136
Coconino Cycle Club	141
Hotel and Tents — Grand Cañon	148
Going to the Grand Cañon	154
Scene on the Hance Trail	160
Grand Cañon Stages at Flagstaff	162

FLAGSTAFF, ARIZONA — GATEWAY TO THE GRAND CAÑON OF THE COLORADO RIVER.

FLAGSTAFF, ARIZONA.

THE GATEWAY TO THE GRAND CAÑON OF THE COLORADO RIVER.

Nestling at the base of the San Francisco Mountains, and protected from Boreas's biting blasts by vast forests of pines, is Flagstaff, the county seat of Coconino County, or, as it has been very appropriately termed, "The Skylight City." It is a thriving town of about three thousand inhabitants, situated on the main line of the Santa Fe Pacific Railroad, which runs in connection with the Great Santa Fe system, whose branches reach out in every direction from the Eastern States to the Pacific Coast.

G. K. WOODS,

The gentlemanly Manager of the Grand Cañon Stage Line, to whom all letters for information on the Grand Cañon — stage and hotel rates, etc. — are respectfully referred.

TO THE TRAVELING PUBLIC.

The following compilation, taken from the Visitor's Book of Captain John Hance, the famous guide of the Grand Cañon, covers a period of ten years. It is put into book form under the immediate supervision of G. K. Woods, General Manager of the Grand Cañon Stage Line, and is now on sale at his office in Flagstaff, Arizona. It is not written by G. K. Woods, but is made up from the actual sentiments of a few of the many visitors to the Grand Cañon in the past ten years. These expressions, the reader will readily understand, are the ideas of the visitors, impressed upon their minds after viewing the Grand Cañon, and written by them individually in the Visitor's Book, from which these data are taken. No well-known European or American writer could under any circumstance give as vivid a description of the grandeur of the panoramic scenery of the Grand Cañon as is furnished by G. K. Woods's book, set forth by the hands of hundreds of visitors from all parts of the United States and Europe. Many of the names the reader will readily recognize. Further than what the following pages furnish nothing need be said of this region of the Grand Cañon. Tourists on a transcontinental tour, besides enjoying the many comforts and privileges granted by the Atchison, Topeka & Santa Fe Railroad Company, are allowed stop-over privileges at Flagstaff, Arizona, giving ample opportunity to take in the beauties of the Grand Cañon of the Colorado and the panoramic frontier scenery of the country from Flagstaff to that wonderful region. The trip can be made by the latest mode of transportation,--" The Auto-Mobile Carriage,"--or by the well-tried and thoroughly reliable Concord coach, which is the chief equipment of J. Wilbur Thurbur's Grand Cañon Stage Line.

After five years of careful observation from many points of the Grand Cañon, I dedicate this work to the traveling public, with the assurance that the original expressions exist; and it will give me pleasure to produce them at any time they may be called fo at Flagstaff, Arizona Territory.   G. K. WOODS.

COLORADO RIVER — FOOT OF GRAND VIEW TRAIL.

THE GRAND CAÑON OF THE COLORADO RIVER.
By J. Curtis Wasson.

From Flagstaff, the point at which tourists leave the Santa Fe system, for the Grand Cañon of the Colorado, at 7 A.M., our stage and six goes out within the folds of the towering pines of the great Coconino Forest, driving through parks lately made verdant by the summer showers, until we have belted the base of the great San Francisco Mountains—the highest and most picturesque of all the ranges in the Southwest—mountains upon whose summits may be seen the perpetual snows, and from whose heights may be had the most extensive view in the West, and the most beautiful in all the ranges of the Rockies—most extensive, because of the atmospheric conditions, as attested by the establishment of the Lowell Observatory here—most beautiful, on account of the varied coloring in the geological formations.

Arriving at Little Springs Station, where a new relay of horses is added, we make haste until the half-way station is reached, passing through a fine unbroken forest of *Pinus ponderosa*, quaking aspen, balsam fir, and spruce. The clear, open forest, the waving grasses, the gorgeously colored mountain flowers, the occasional chirp of the forest songsters, the clear, ice-cold springs traversing our smooth compact road, the peaks, clear-cut, cold, and massive, towering up nearly 14,000 feet into the blue above, with now and then a band of mountain deer bounding speedily around some curve, like enchanted sprites from fairyland, the low rumbling of our great Concord stage, the sound of two dozen hoofs, the sharp crack of the driver's whip, the clear, cold, bracing atmosphere, every breath of which seems to stimulate, the indescribably beautiful Painted Desert outstretching for a hundred miles to our right,—amid such environments as these one may revel in the wonders of Nature and feel the magic touch of her hand divine—for here indeed is a drive ideal, amid scenes real, grandly austere, yet inspiringly touched by the sweetest of her graces.

One fain would linger on scenes like these but we have arrived at Cedar Station, and after partaking of a very refreshing luncheon we are given a new relay of horses and hasten over the desert portion of our ride to Moqui Station, where another relay is provided, which takes us to the Cañon Hotel, at the rim of the cañon, where we arrive at 7 o'clock P. M.

Leaving our Concord stage, giving our grips to the porter, not even waiting for "facial ablutions," we hasten across the yard and up to the rim of the cañon, when, looking over—the Chasm of the Creator, the Gulf of God, the Erosion of the Ages, lies in all its awfulness before us,—awful, yet grand; appalling, yet attractive; awe inspiring, yet fascinating in its greetings.

To speak of its dimensions as being 240 miles long, 12 to 15 miles wide, and 6,000 feet in depth, conveys no idea of the Grand Cañon. One must read to enjoy, see to appreciate, and examine to realize this, the greatest scenic attraction in the world.

But little is absolute, much is relative, and for this reason extent can not be appreciated in the Grand Cañon. When we are told that the opposite rim, which seems but a pistol-shot away, is over fifteen miles from where we are standing, we are amazed. When we are told that down a little to our left, where may be outlined but dimly a small mound, our eyes behold a mountain over 1,600 feet high; when we are told that the white sheet of water to be seen far down the cañon, seemingly but a mere brook over which one might step with ease, is nearly 600 feet in width; when we are told that yon two pedestals which barely jut out above the basic Cliff are over 600 feet in height; when we are told these truths and many more which might be added, no wonder that our eyes seem to apologize, and our judgment is "relegated for repairs,"—no wonder that we are awed by the enormous proportions, and the mighty magnitude of this Awful Abyss!

Although our eyes and judgment may need to be readjusted

that we may appreciate the extent of this "erosive entity," yet the soul never fails to respond to the entrancing charm and fascinating beauty of this scene of scenes, this phenomenon of phenomena.

There is a triune strata of the cañon, ranging from the limestone formation above, with all its graduated colors, variegated from a mottled sable to an ermine white, the dark juttings being grim imaginary statues typical of Pluto's realm, but counterbalanced by the statues standing here and there, lapped and overlapped, by the soft white folds left by the erosion of centuries, and typical of the heraldry of a summer clime and a kindlier kin, extending into the ruddy sandstone beneath, whose granulated formation invites that sculptor of the ages — Erosion — who wields her wand o'er her handmaids of wind and water, and asks naught for the execution of her mandates but cycles—cycles of time—and her wish is granted.

This sandstone formation continues down to the granite, whose massive solidity seems a typical base upon which to rest a mile of statuary—peaks, promontories, and mountains.

Upon all this fancy the added beauty of the immortal glory of a sunset glow, whose variegated colors, hues, and tints resolve one into another, playing, dancing, reveling in the scenic harvest like fairies whose setting sun must sound their knell of doom, now growing bolder, keener, deeper, richer, only to again retreat to be combined once more.

The sun sinks in the west, when the colors, bidding each other good-night, whirl as if in courtesy, and recede from sight. Their going has left us the poorer. Whom did they enrich? None, save the fantasies of memory.

Lost in revelry, we do not notice that the moon, whose beams even now, using each projecting butte as a dim lantern from which to reflect its glimmering, quivering light, has risen in the east.

We then return to the Grand Cañon Hotel, built upon its rim, and after enjoying its luxurious service, alternated by various trips down the several trails, we go back to Flagstaff, by the Grand Cañon stage route, which, I am free to say, gives the swiftest and best service of any route in the Southwest.

GRANDEUR RIDGE — ON THE GRAND VIEW TRAIL.

NOTICE TO THE READER

The pages which follow contain the ideas of a few of the many hundreds of visitors who have visited the Grand Cañon over the Atchison, Topeka & Santa Fe Route, via Flagstaff, Arizona. The reader will note that some of the writers reside in Arizona, but most of the visitors are from other portions of the United States and from Europe. Many of the tourists who have herein expressed themselves are well-known pleasure-seekers and admirers of Nature in her grandest forms. They have visited such points of interest as the Alps in Switzerland, the various attractions in Germany, the Highlands of Scotland, have seen the sparkling waters of the Thames, England, the Giant's Causeway in Ireland,—but have not kissed the blarney-stone. They concede that while America, from a scenic standpoint, has many beauties — the great Niagara Falls, the Yellowstone Park in Montana, the Natural Bridge in Virginia, the Yosemite Valley in California, with its Mirror Lake and grand peaks — all these sink into insignificance when compared with Nature's greatest attraction, the Grand Cañon of the Colorado.

PERSONAL IMPRESSIONS
OF THE
GRAND CAÑON OF THE COLORADO RIVER.

April 16–20, 1891.

GIFFORD PINCHOB,
      New York.

Went to the river. Time from head of trail to river and back to head of trail, 9 hours and 55 minutes.

April 20, 1891.

J. M. SIMPSON,

The world hath many sights for the tourist and recreation seeker to look upon, but none therein contained, begin to compare with the Grand Cañon of the Colorado River, as seen seventy miles north of Flagstaff, Arizona.

CHARLES G. THOMAS,
  AND WIFE, **Chicago, Ill.**

Arrived May 15, 1891; remained two days.

H. P. ALDRICH AND WIFE,
    Albuquerque, N. M.

Arrived May 15, 1891; remained two days.

May 15, 1891.

M. J. KEYS, Correspondent,
  St. Joseph (Mo.) Gazette.

Went to the river. Time from head of trail, 9 hours, 26 minutes.

M. H. POST, M. D.
     St. Louis, Mo.

Arrived May 16th, left 18th; went to cabin in Cañon 17th.

May 18, 1891.

E. S. WILCOX, Flagstaff,
      Arizona.

May 20, 1891.

CHARLEY GREENLAW,
    Flagstaff, Arizona.

May 20, 1891.

Mrs. GEO. T. DORNLIFF,
      Illinois.

I can cheerfully say that this, the Grand Cañon of the Colorado River, is the grandest sight of my life — as I noticed in this little book of Capt. John Hance, a great many people say indescribable. I can say nothing more. It is beyond reason to think of describing it in any way. You must see it to appreciate it. A grand sight of this kind and so few people know of it. By accident I formed the acquaintance of two ladies en route to the Grand Cañon. I joined them. We have enjoyed our trip; the stage ride from Flagstaff to the Grand Cañon is grand. Good horses, competent and accommodating drivers. I have seen the Yosemite, have visited California several different times, in fact seen all the principal points of interest in the United States, but the most wonderful, awe-inspiring piece of Nature's own work is this, the Grand Cañon of the Colorado River.

May 20, 1891.
    JOHN DONAHUE,
            Flagstaff, Arizona.

May 20, 1891.
    H. HELLER,
            Flagstaff, Arizona.

May 22, 1891.
    E. RANDOLPH,
            Red Horse, Arizona.

May 22, 1891.
    F. L. ARMSTRONG,
            Red Horse, Arizona.

JOHN C. FURMAN,
            New York.

ROBERT GRAWSHAY,
            London, England.
    Arrived May 23; left 24, 1891; and very sorry to have so little time.

LAWRENCE FERRIER,
    (Via New York,)
            Edinburgh, Scotland.

A. C. MORSE,
            Flagstaff, Arizona.

J. A. HARRISON,
            Chicago, Ill.

May 24, 1891.
    JAMES S. CRAWFORD,
            Ayr, Scotland.

May 25, 1891.
    CHARLES W. MERRILL
    AND WIFE,   Indianapolis.

May 25, 1891.
    HERMAN D. OLESON,
            Sweden.

I travel thousands of miles every year, and think I have seen all the sights of the world. I have been traveling for the past ten years. The Grand Cañon of the Colorado River is the most wonderful piece of work I have ever seen. Myself and Capt. John Hance have been going for two days. Into the cañon the first day, the rim the second. The most beautiful view I think is from Moran Point. Let me advise all to take one of the Captain's horses in going to the river. Thanking the good people at this hotel and Capt. Hance, I bid you all good-by.

O. J. HODGE,
VIRGINIA SHEDD HODGE,
            Cleveland, Ohio.

Arrived May 27; departed May 29, 1891. We have seen the Yosemite, the Yellowstone, Mt. Hood, Mt. Blanc, and traveled through Alaska, but never saw anything so grand, so sublime, and so marvelous as the Grand Cañon of the Colorado River from this point. God bless our friend John Hance!

May 29, 1891.

ALFRED L. DICKENSON,
   Flagstaff, Arizona.

June 1, 1891.

Mrs. D. ROBERTS,
   New York.

My trip has been a pleasant one to the Grand Cañon. The cañon itself is beautiful. The immensity and grandeur of this cañon cannot be appreciated unless you see it. No one has any idea of its greatness till once you stand on the rim and look down upon this wonderful piece of Nature's own work.

June 3, 1891.

HARRY L. YOUNG,
MAY J. YOUNG,
   Shamokin, Pa.

GEO. A. CLARK,
   Minneapolis, Minn.

Arrived June 2; left June 4, 1891.

J. B. SMITH,
   Flagstaff, Arizona.

Arrived June 2; departed June 4, 1891.

June 10, 1891.

Mrs. J. C. STREETER,
   Boston.

Nature's own work is most beautiful. I can scarcely believe my own eyes. I can say nothing. The Grand Cañon is here. Come and see it for yourself. You cannot be disappointed. So far beyond my expectations. Captain John Hance is here, too. He will interest you if the cañon does n't.

Thursday, June 11, 1891.

JULES BAUMANN, Artist,
   Prescott, Arizona.

D. T. McDOUGLE, U. S.,
  Botanist,
   La Fayette, Ind.

Thursday, June 11, 1891.

JAMES L. STONE,
   Missouri.

CAL. OSBON,

Born Nov. 20, 1849, in Indiana; went to California in 1874; then to Oregon; 1877, back to California, 1884; went to Tucson, Arizona, landed in Flagstaff, Arizona, 1891. I make views as a specialty of Arizona. I have views all down the trail to the falls.

Mr. and Mrs. J. EUGENE BROWNING,
  78 Cotton Exchange,
   New York City.

Arrived June 16; left June 18, 1891.

June 18, 1891.

N. J. CAMERON,
   Flagstaff, Arizona.

June 24, 1891.
  J. M. CLARK,
      Flagstaff, Arizona.

June 24, 1891.
  W. R. WORTH,
      Flagstaff, Arizona.

  T. A. PARSONS,
  J. M. PARSONS,
  CHAS. PARSONS,
      All of St. Louis, Mo.

1891.
  WALTER DOUGLASS,
      99 John St., N. Y.
  ALEX. MACKENZIE,
      11 Clift St., N. Y.
  Commercial Mining Company.

1891.
  AUGUST J. BOWIE,
      San Francisco, Cal.

July 18, 1891.
  J. H. WRIGHT,
      New York City.

  F. N. BARRETT,
      New York City.

  CHAS. L. RICKERSON,
      Arizona.

  CHAS. E. RICKERSON,
      New York.

  JAMES M. FARRAR,
      Brooklyn, N. Y.

  CORA A. SMITH,
      Brooklyn, N. Y.
  Went down into cañon July 19, 1891.

  DAISY SIMPSON,
      Montreal, Canada.
  Went down into cañon July 19, 1891.

  CELIN JEANNETTE BARRETT,
      New York.
  Down into the cañon July 19 and 20, 1891.

  LEWIS D. BOUCHER,
      Sherbrooke, P. Q., Canada.

1891.
  GEO. W. McADAMS,
      Ellington Lake.

July 21, 1891.
  CHAS. COLLINS,
      Springfield, Mo.

July 21, 1891.
  PABLO A. GARCIA.

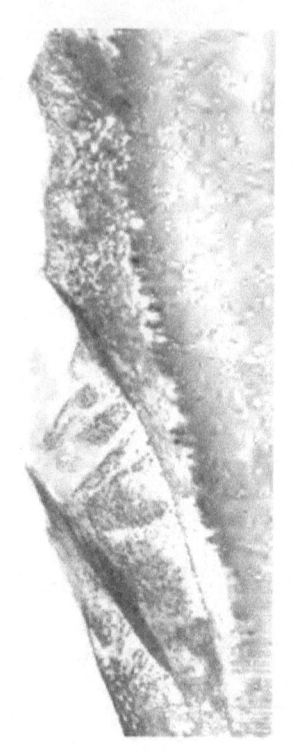

Over the falls at midnight.
The lost, strayed, or stolen party.
Arrived on July 21, 1891; left on July 24, 1891.

L. H. WRIGHT,
                Philadelphia, Pa.
MARY KELLAM,
                Los Angeles, Cal.
ARLETTA BRODE,
                Buda, Ill.
LAURA HOXWORTH,
                Flagstaff, Arizona.
IRENE HOXWORTH,
                Flagstaff, Arizona.
S. N. PECK,
                Phœnix, Arizona.
J. R. LOCKETT,
                Flagstaff, Arizona.
E. A. SLIKER,
                Cincinnati, O.
Chaperoned by Mrs. J. F. DAGGS,
                Flagstaff, Arizona.

Oh, what fun at the last falls! Ask any of the party about it.

A. NELSON,
                Flagstaff, Arizona.

August 9, 1891.
D. P. HOOKER,
                Flagstaff, Arizona.

WM. MERRELL,
                Leavenworth, Kan.

Went down in cañon with D. P. Hooker, August 10, 1891, to cabin, and returned same day. Mr. Merrell's age is eighty years.

F. FAIRCHILDS,
                Flagstaff, Arizona.

August 16, 1891.
THEO. F. HOLDEN,
                Flagstaff, Arizona.

August 16, 1891.
GEO. B. JOHNSON,
                Flagstaff, Arizona.

August 16, 1891.
HELENA JOHNSON,
                Flagstaff, Arizona.

August 16, 1891.
ELIZABETH HOLDEN,
                Flagstaff, Arizona.

August 16, 1891.
W. F. HULL.

First entered the cañon June 22, 1884; June 26, 1884, commenced surveying road from cañon to Cedar Ranch, in company with Silas Ruggles and John Hance. First visit to the cañon in February, 1880.
I. O. O. F., K. of P., F. A. M.

August 17, 1891.
GEO. R. DECAMP.

This is the greatest sight on earth. I have seen almost everything in the way of cañons, but this beats them all. You will have to see it; no one can tell you about it.

August 18, 1891.
  D. E. ISABELLE,
  E. M. ISABELLE,
  Mrs. M. W. HALL,
    All of Flagstaff, Arizona.

August 19, 1891.
  M. F. GENNINGS.

  Miss HARRIETT COLTON,
    Brooklyn, N. Y.

  FLORENCE N. DUKES,
    Brooklyn, N. Y.

  EMMA SPALDING,
    Prescott, Arizona.

  ALICE METZ,
    Cincinnati, Ohio.

  Lieut. G. H. MORGAN, U. S. A.,
    Late of Texas.

  Mrs. WM. CARROLL,
    Flagstaff, Arizona.

JOHN DONOVON,
  Flagstaff, Arizona.

C. E. HOWARD,
  Flagstaff, Arizona.

P. H. HOLT,
  Flagstaff, Arizona.

August 19, 1891.
  Mr. and Mrs. G. W. MEYLERT,
  Mr. and Mrs. A. A. KEEN,
  Mrs. ANDREW SMITH,
  Miss LILLIAN HIRST,
    Albuquerque.
  Mrs. T. J. WOODSIDE,
    El Paso.
  Mrs. S. S. PRATT,
    Brooklyn, N. Y.
  L. M. LATTA,
    Bluewater, N. Y.
  H. PERKINS,
    Holbrook, Arizona.
  Chaperoned by
    Mrs. G. W. MEYLERT.

Left for Flagstaff on the morning of August 21, 1891.

August 21, 1891.
  Mr. and Mrs. G. T. HAYES.

  We have enjoyed our trip. It is worth seeing. Wish we could stay a week. The grandest sight of our lives.

August 21, 1891.

Mr. and Mrs. F. FAIRCHILDS
AND FAMILY,
    Flagstaff, Arizona.

J. C. GRIM,
Mrs. J. C. GRIM,
FRED GRIM,
BURTON GRIM,
CLARA GRIM,
LILLIE JONES,
    All of Flagstaff, Arizona.

August 30, 1891.

GEO. McCORMICK,
    Flagstaff, Arizona.

A. J. COOPER,
GEO. SMITH,
D. K. TRIPP,
    All of Chicago, Ill.

August 30, 1891.

J. W. WATSON,
    1st Lieut. 10th Cavalry,
    Ft. Bayard, N. M.

August 30, 1891.

J. W. HEARDY,
    First Lieut. 3d U. S. Cavalry,
    San Antonio, Texas.

August 30, 1891.

F. G. IRWIN,
    First Lieut. Second U. S. Cavalry,
    Fort Bowie, Arizona.

August 31, 1891.

M. R. PETERSON,
    Second Lieut. Tenth Infantry,
    Fort Wingate, N. M.

August 31, 1891.

EUGENE HARLOW,
    From Johnnie Bull's Islands.

Visited the cañon and all trails, in company with Captain Hance. Very grand, and I think I shall show my good sense not trying to descend this unique cañon of the earth.

J. W. POWERS,
    Washington, D. C.

D. M. RIORDAN,
    Flagstaff, Arizona.

September 26, 1891.

MARY CAROLINE HUGHES,
    Cambridge, Eng.
Dr. FRITZ FRECH,
    Berlin, Germany.
Dr. WRIFINZ,
    Tubingen, Germany.
Dr. D. MARCHAND,
    Photo Artist London "Graphic."
Dr. Baron SIBNEY WOHRMANN HOLHEN,
    Livonia, Germany.
Dr. A. BOTPLETZ,
    Municha, Germany.

Dr. H. CREDNER,
    Leipzig, Germany.
Dr. JOHANNES WALTHER,
    Feria, Germany.
Dr. RUDOLF CRIDNER,
    Germany.
Dr. A. ULRICH,
    Strasburg, Deutchland.
H. M. CADELL,
    Grange Boness, Scotland.
WILLARD D. JOHNSON,
    Washington, D. C.
ALFRED HARKER,
WM. KERNEY HUGHES,
    Cambridge, England.
Dr. AUG. STRENG,
    Professor from Giessen, Ger.
Dr. D. J. BRANNEN,
    Flagstaff, Arizona.
Dr. JOHN R. HAYNES,
    Los Angeles, Cal.
Dr. GEO. V. J. BERINE,
    Halle A. L., Germany.
F. PLIENINGER,
—— KAYSER,
    Marburg, Germany.
I. ROMBURG,
    Berlin, Germany.
Dr. CARL DIERMER,
    Vienna, Austria.
H. TOLLIEZ,
    Professor University Lausanne,
    Switzerland.
ERNEST VANDEN BROEK,
    Buinelles, Belgieque.
MORZ LOHERTSIEGE,
    Belgieque.

Dr. V. ZITTEL,
    Municha, Germany.
E. De MARGERIE,
    Paris, France.
Dr. BURGEART,
    "Mente et Malleo,"
    Munchen, Bayern.

The above parties belonging to the International Geological Congress.

Dr. GEO. H. POWERS,
CORNELIA C. POWERS,
    San Francisco, Cal.

Mrs. A. D. MARCHAND,
Mr. A. D. MARCHAND,
    268 S. Main Street,
    Los Angeles, Cal.

September, 1891.
    E. R. HERMAN,
        California.

By all means visit the Grand Cañon of the Colorado River, in Arizona. See Hance, too.

October 3, 1891.
    Mrs. GEO. WINFIELD ROOPE,
        Boston, Mass.

October 3, 1891.
    C. C. HITCHCOCK,
    M. E. HITCHCOCK,
        Ware, Mass.

We repeat the sentiment expressed by O. J. Hodge, that "we have visited the Yosemite, the Yellowstone, Mt. Hood, Mt. Blanc, and traveled through Alaska,

COTTONWOOD CAÑON—LOOKING NORTH ON GRAND VIEW TRAIL

but never saw anything so grand, so sublime, and so marvelous as the Grand Cañon of the Colorado, from this point. God bless our friend John Hance."

A. H. SMUTZ,
                    Fresno, Cal.

October 5, 1891.

C. C. HITCHCOCK.

Left head of trail for river at 6:40 A.M., reached Hance's cabin, 7:55 A.M.; arrived at Colorado River, 10 A.M.; started on return trip, 10:35 A.M.; arrived at cabin; 12:55 P.M.; left cabin, 1:15 P.M.; arrived at head of trail 4:22 P.M. Time, nine hours and forty-two minutes.

October 5, 1891.

G. E. TUTTLE.

Talk about holes in the ground,—well, this is one of them. I have been in the cañon to-day. Don't intend to go in any more. I am completely out of anything to say. Come and see it for yourselves. No one can tell you about it. I have seen the world, but had not seen near all of it, until I saw this cañon. Farewell, Captain; am coming again. Will bring a party with me next time. Thanks for your kindness, etc.

October 13, 1891.

JOHN T. WALLACE,
                    Monte Vista, Colo.

October 13, 1891.

O. S. GARNER,
                    Massachusetts.

Of all the sights in the world this is the greatest sight I ever have seen. Words cannot tell the grandeur, beauty, immensity, and sublimity of this wonderful production of Nature's own work. I would advise all tourists to visit this cañon. You cannot be disappointed. The beautiful forests we travel through going to the cañon is worth the trip alone. I am coming again to stop here for a month. I have visited many places, but this beats them all. Good-by. O. S. G.

November 7, 1891.

Mr. F. J. HOCHDERFFER,
Mrs. F. J. HOCHDERFFER,
ROSE HOCHDERFFER,
EMMA HOCHDERFFER,
ROCK HOCHDERFFER,
CLEVELAND HOCHDERFFER,
                    Of Flagstaff, Arizona.

April 9, 1892.

First of the Season.

HORACE C. HOVEY,
                    Middletown, Conn.

Intended to come last fall with Geological Congress, but am contented to open the ball for 1892, "Mente et Malleo," as special correspondent of *Scientific American*. Went down Hance trail with Mr. Boucher, and stayed over night, returning next day; enjoyed it immensely. Found the trail in excellent order, and made the trip comfortably.

April 9, 1892.
    JOHN J. TRILTON
                New Mexico.

Arrived here all O. K. Went up to the rim of cañon; was far beyond my expectations. Of all the grand sights in the world this is one of them. I have visited in Europe, Alaska, have seen the Yellowstone, all the different places in California, but nothing comes up to this. No one could tell you of it. No language could ever tell you the grandeur, the beauty, the immensity of this wonderful cañon. I would like to have all my friends here at this hour to view this, Nature's own work, with me. Farewell, Captain; I hope to see you again.

April 14, 1892.
    Mr. and Mrs. MARSHALL,
    Miss F. E. MARSHALL,
    C. M. MARSHALL,
            All of Flagstaff, Arizona.

April 15, 1892.
    T. A. RIORDAN,
            Flagstaff, Arizona.

April 15, 1892.
    T. R. GABLE,
            Albuquerque, N. M.

April 18, 1892.
        The John D. Hoff Abestos Co.
    By JOHN D. HOFF,
            Of San Diego, Cal.

JOHN I. McCOOK,
            New York, N. Y.

ARCHIBALD ALEXANDER,
            New York.

MAITLAND ALEXANDER,
            New York, N. Y.

C. CHARMLEY,
            Chicago, Ill.

SAMUEL COLMAN,
            Newport, Rhode Island.

JOHN J. LARKIN,
            St. Paul, Minn.

LOUIS SPEARS,
I. F. WHEELER,
            Flagstaff, Arizona.

May 12, 1892.
    WM. CAREY,
        Colonel H. B. M., Royal Artillery,
        "Retired" (Cox & Co.)
            London, England.

May 17, 1892.
    T. G. DANIELLS,
    F. W. VAN SICKLEN,
    W. A. BISSEL,
    G. P. REYNOLDS,
            All of Alameda, Cal.

May 17, 1892.
 J. H. HOSKINS, Jr.,
    Flagstaff, Arizona.

May 21, 1892.
 HERMAN WESTERMAN,
    Cincinnati, Ohio.

 J. S. BUNNELL,
    San Francisco, Cal.

 W. F. CLARKE,
    New York.

 CHAS. F. LUMMIS,
    Isleta, N. M.

May 24, 1892.
 W. H. JACKSON,
    Denver, Colo.

May 24, 1892.
 T. MORAN,
    New York.

May 24, 1892.
 C. A. HIGGINS,
    Chicago, Ill.

May 24, 1892.
 PAUL N. MORAN,
    New York.

May 24, 1892.
 SAM C. TAYLOR,
    Denver, Colo.

 ALBERT MAGEE AND WIFE,
 I. R. BAXLEY AND WIFE,
    All of Santa Barbara, Cal.

 I could hope that those who come to the cañon would get Hance to show them something of what he knows, and that is more than can be suspected simply on the first outlook. Much of my intense pleasure I owe to him.   I. R. B.

 J. GARNETT AND DAUGHTERS,
 HAROLD ECCLER,
    London, England.

 E. B. REYNOLDS,
 E. A. REYNOLDS,
    South Bend, Indiana.

 Arrived June 10; left June 12, 1892.

June 14, 1892.
 I. S. GOFORTH,
    Georgetown, N. M.

June 14, 1892.
 G. B. INGRAM,
    Fayetteville, Arkansas.

June 16, 1892.
 GEO. PRIME,
    Flagstaff, Arizona.

June 13, 1892.
    H. H. WATKINS,
    Mrs. H. H. WATKINS,
            Kingman, Ariz.

June 13, 1892.
    S. T. ELLIOTT,
    Mrs. S. T. ELLIOTT,
            Flagstaff, Arizona.

June 13, 1892.
    J. M. MARSHALL,
            Flagstaff, Arizona.

June 13, 1892.
    Mrs. A. T. CORNISH,
            Flagstaff, Arizona.

June 13, 1892.
    A. A. ALLESTER,
            Flagstaff, Arizona.

June 13, 1892.
    ANNIE L. ROSS,
            Flagstaff, Ariz.

June 13, 1892.
    S. L. ROUSH,
            Eldon, Iowa.

June 13, 1892.
    ROBERT McCANN,
            Flagstaff, Arizona.

June 13, 1892.
    SAMUEL BAXTER,
            Flagstaff, Ariz.

June 14, 1892.
    ALICE WAINWRIGHT,
            St. Louis, Mo.
    RUSSELL H. MONRO,
    EMLIE MONRO,
            Market Harboro, England.
    WM. B. DOWD,
    CHAS. T. WING,
            New York City.
    All with the *AI* cattle outfit.

June 15, 1892.
    R. C. DRYDEN,
            Winslow, Ariz.

June 15, 1892.
    F. W. SMITH,
            Winslow, Ariz.

    C. C. TILLSON,
            Pueblo, Colo.

    WM. SHROYER,
            Flagstaff, Ariz.

    GEO. K. SMITH,
            Phoenix, Arizona.

    FRED GOODRICH,
            Phoenix, Arizona.

HORSESHOE POINT—ON THE GRAND VIEW TRAIL, NORTH

VIC. E. HANNY,
    Phoenix, Arizona.

June 28, 1892.
 GEO. MARSHALL,
    Syracuse, N. Y.

I arrived at Flagstaff on the 25th of June, 1892, from Syracuse, N. Y., and started on the 26th of June for the Grand Cañon of the Colorado by stage line. After riding all day through some of the largest forests of pines, and the most beautiful valleys that I have ever seen, I arrived at the cañon just when the sun was setting. On the morning of June 27th, myself and several others were guided over the trail and into the cañon by Captain John Hance. After winding around here and there over the trail for several miles, we reached the river, which is a grand sight. After resting an hour, and a plunge in the river, we started for the rim, arriving about dusk. I have traveled over the United States, have seen about all the sights, but I have never seen such a wonderful and marvelous piece of nature's own work as this, the Grand Cañon of the Colorado River.

June 28, 1892.
 Rev. N. F. NORTON,
 Rev. E. G. POOLER AND WIFE.

June 30, 1892.
 D. K. TRIPP,
    Chicago, Ill.

June 30, 1892.
JAMES KASSON,
    St. Paul, Minn.

June 30, 1892.
R. C. JEFFERSON,
    St. Paul, Minn.

July 5, 1892.
A. NEALON.

July 5, 1892.
E. CAMPBELL.

HAL C. WYMAN,
GLADYS WYMAN.
    Detroit, Mich.

JOS. B. VERKAMP,
    Cincinnati.

W. BABBITT,
    Flagstaff, A. T.

July 8, 1892.
H. T. SMITH,
    Prescott, A. T.

Miss MADIE CHRISMAN,
    Portland, Or.

Come June 22, 1892, Summer at Grand Cañon.

July 9, 1892.

Mrs. JOHN Z. T. VARMER.

I have never witnessed anything like this. It scares me to even try to look down into it. My God, I am afraid the whole country will fall into this great hole in the ground.

July 10, 1892.

Rev. ROBERT COLTMAN,
    Pastor 1st Presbyterian church,
M. J. COLTMAN,
JENNIE R. COLTMAN,
                    Flagstaff, A. T.

July 10, 1892.

BLANCH METZ,
                    Cincinnati, O.

July 10, 1892.

J. C. SANCHEZ,
                    Milton, A. T.

July 10, 1892.

JOHN H. HICKS,
                    Milton, A. T.

July 10, 1892.

MOLLIE CLEMMENTS,
                    Baltimore, Md.

A. WALGREEN,
                    Lapland, Sweden.

J. W. TOUMEY,
E. O. WOOTON, Botanist,

Botanical and Entomological party, from experiment stations at Tucson, Ariz., and Las Cruces, N. M.

H. H. SWARTHOUT,
                    Anderson, Mich.

R. R. LARKINS,
                    Las Cruces, N. M.

CLAWRENCE T. HAGERTY,
                    Las Cruces, N. M.

C. H. TYLER TOWNSEND,
    Entomologist exper. stn.
                    Las Cruces, N. M.

A. B. CORDLEY,
    Asst. U. S. Entomologist,
                    Washington, D. C.

July 12, 1892.

GERTRUDE B. STEVENS.

This is a warm place. I fainted when I saw this awful looking cañon. I never wanted a drink so bad in my life. Captain, I won't forget you for bringing me the oyster-can full of water. Good-by.

Mrs. JOHN T. CHARMER.

The grandest, the most wonderful, the greatest sight on earth. I can never forget it. Visit the Grand Cañon of the Colorado River.

E. S. GOSNEY,
   Flagstaff, A. T.

WM. WINCUP AND WIFE,
   Los Angeles, Cal.

M. S. NORMAN AND WIFE,
Miss JESSIE NORMAN,
   St. Joe, Mo.

C. W. NOYES AND WIFE,
   Boston, Mass.

Miss R. J. MACY,
   Los Angeles.

C. E. HOLLAND,
   Phoenix, A. T.

O. A. TURNER,
   Madison, now of Phoenix.

BEN DONEY,
Mrs. DONEY,
BENNIE DONEY,
   Flagstaff, Arizona.

MARY QUINN,
   Flagstaff, A. T.

JOHN WESLEY LEANDDER,
   Texas.

C. W. HARDY,
   Cleveland, Ohio.

R. H. CRAWFORD,
   Toronto, Ont., C.

July, 1892.

HENRY B. THORN.
Hurrah for the Cañon and John Hance.

July 13, 1892.

OLIVER S. WESTCOTT,
Principal North Division High School, Chicago.

Mrs. ELIONER O. WESTCOTT,
   Chicago.

J. W. FLANDERS,
Traveler for J. C. Ayer & Co.

F. B. HIGGINS,
   Greenville, S. C.

J. B. STEINMETZ,
   New Paris, Ind.

July 14, 1892.

HENRY R. WADE.
By Joe! this cañon takes the whole shooting-match.

July 15, 1892.

　Mrs. G. P. PETERS.

　I have visited the whole world. I travel nine months in the year. I have never seen anything so grand as a sunset view of the Grand Cañon of the Colorado River.

July 16, 1892.

　C. M. FUNSTON,
　　　　Editor Coconino Sun,
　Mrs. C. M. FUNSTON,
　MARY FUNSTON,
　HELEN FUNSTON,
　HANNAH FUNSTON,
　　　　All of Flagstaff, Ariz.

　MELIE E. LOWRY,
　　　　Indianapolis, Indiana.

　MARY SMITH.

　Our crowd, ladies and all, made trip from cabin to river, back to cabin and up to head of trail in one day. According to Mr. Hance, beating the record made by ladies.

　M. M. CROCKER, M. D.,
　Mrs. M. M. CROCKER,
　　　　Ft. Mojave, Arizona.

　LUCY STILLWELL,
　　　　Ft. Mojave, Ariz.
　JULIA STILLWELL,
　　　　Cuba, Mo.

July 20, 1892.

　Mrs. AMANDA LOCKETT,
　　69 yrs. old.
　H. C. LOCKETT,
　Miss ROSA CLARK,
　Mrs. E. F. GREENLAW,
　　Four of us and no more of us.
　　　　Flagstaff, Arizona.

　J. J. WEIMER,
　　　　Winslow, A. T.

　MINNIE VANPELT,
　　　　Chicago, Ill.

　VIOLA F. STEKEY,
　　　　Greenfield, O.

　F. A. GULLY AND WIFE,
　　　　Tucson, Ariz.

　C. B. COLLINGWOOD,
　　　　Tucson, Ariz.

July 22, 1892.

　M. T. WARDEN.

　This is the spot of all spots on earth. I would like to locate on this spot for about a year.

THE MODE OF TRAVEL IN THE GRAND CAÑON.

July 24, 1892.

    EDITH ALVORD,
    BELL SWITZER,
    LULA GRAHAM,
    Mrs. W. A. SWITZER,
    W. H. SWITZER,
    BURT CAMERON,
    H. J. RAND,
    STANLEY SYKES,
        All of Flagstaff, Ariz.

July 29, 1892.

    M. M. KIRKMAN AND PARTY.
    Mr. M. W. KIRK,
    Dr. W. J. HAWKS,
    Mr. ARCHIBALD McNEAL,
    Mr. A. T. McCORMICK,
        The unsuspecting profit.
    Master A. T. KIRKMAN,
    Master M. J. KIRKMAN.

July 29, 1892.

    F. F. JAQUES,
        Kansas City, Mo.

Sunday, July 30, 1892.

    E. P. S. ANDREWS AND WIFE,
    Mrs. H. P. HINE,
    JERRY MILLAY AND WIFE,
    LEON BOUVIER,
        All of Phoenix, Arizona.

    ALEX LEE MARCHANT, B. A.,
        London, England.

August 1, 1892.

    W. E. THORNE,
        Kansas City, Mo.

August 4, 1892.

    HARRY E. WOOD,
        Kansas City, Mo.

August 4, 1892.

    N. B. McDOWELL,
        Cleveland, Ohio.

    FRANK RUMSEY,
        Flagstaff, Arizona.

August 4, 1892.

    JAMES E. LAVELLE,
        Albuquerque, N. M.

August 4, 1892.

    CHAS. B. BARKER,

    The Grand Cañon is the most wonderful thing I ever looked at. Surely worth seeing.

August 5, 1892.

    J. C. HERNDON,
        Prescott, Ariz.

    T. G. NORRIS,
        Flagstaff, Arizona.

    CHAS. W. HERNDON,
        Prescott, Arizona.

August 5, 1892.

The champion athletic pedestrian visitors, under the auspices of
    WM. McINTIRE,
        Bellemont, Arizona.
Mrs. T. J. GRACE,
Miss GRACE L. GRACE,
Miss MARY PRIME,
Mr. J. WESBY,
    All of Bellemont, A. T.

Miss HATTIE J. HOPSON,
    Washington, D. C.

Miss MARTHA McINTIRE,
    Clay Center, Kansas.

August 12, 1892.
    C. H. SPEERS,
        Asst. G. P. A. A. & P. R. R.
        San Francisco, Cal.

August 12, 1892.
    E. P. GRAY, C. V. R. R.,
        San Francisco, Cal.

August 12, 1892.
    A. E. MARCHAND,
        San Francisco, Cal.

August 12, 1892.
    JOHN F. McCARTHY,
    Formerly of Cincinnati, now of San Francisco, Cal. Wabash R. R.

August 12, 1892.
    H. S. VAN SLYCK,
        A. & P. R. R.
        Albuquerque, N. M.

August 12, 1892.
    Mr. and Mrs. H. G. PATTERSON,
        St. Louis, Mo.

GEO. D. HOOPER,

Captain, I wish I were in your place to view this great cañon every day. One would never get tired of it. What a grand sight.

August 13, 1892.
    J. I. THORNTON,
    Mrs. GEO. F. THORNTON,
        Williams.

August 13, 1892.
    Miss MAY ANDERSON,
        Alabama.

August 13, 1892.
    Miss PERRIN,
    Miss HELEN PERRIN,
    E. B. PERRIN, Jr.,
        San Francisco, Cal.

August 14, 1892.
    E. L. NORRIS,
        Flagstaff, Arizona.

August 14, 1892.
    C. LEWIS,
        Flagstaff, Arizona.

August 14, 1892.
    ED. T. GALE,
            Flagstaff, Arizona.

August 15, 1892.
    Mr. and Mrs. JOSEPH B. CROSBY,
            Boston, Mass.

Arrived at John Hance's summer ranch 7:05 P.M.; leave 6:30 A.M., August 18, 1892.

August 15, 1882.
    Mrs. JOHN R. BARTLETT,
            Providence, R. I.

August 18, 1892.
    BEN SKINNER,
    WM. PATTON,
            Both of Flagstaff, Arizona.

August 18, 1892.
    Mrs. W. H. YANCEY,
    Miss STELLA YANCEY,
            Flagstaff, Arizona.

    Miss SUE RUMSEY,
            Flagstaff, Arizona.

    Mr. ROBERT FREIDLINE,

August 19, 1892.
    L. H. MASSIE,
            Phoenix, Arizona.

August 19, 1892.
    LOY J. BROWN,
        Martinsburg, Audran Co., Mo.

August 19, 1892
    Col. FRANK HULL, Jr.,
        The Grand Cañon is so far more wonderful than Yosemite Valley or Yellowstone Park or any interesting points in the world. It is so grand and beautiful that no pen of any living author can describe it.

August 20, 1892.
    WM. FRANCIS HULL,
    ALICE GERTRUDE HULL,
            Both of San Francisco, Cal.

August 20, 1892.
    SUSIE E. BUSH,
            Albuquerque, N. M.

August 20, 1892.
    Mrs. LISSIE MORRELL,
            Williams, Arizona.

August 20, 1892.
    Mrs. KATE JOHNSTON,
            Williams, Arizona.

August 20, 1892.
    Miss MAUD DICKENSON,
            Williams, Arizona.

August 20, 1892.
    Miss MAUD HILL,
            Albuquerque, N. M.

JOHN WOOD,
  Williams, Arizona.

HENRY C. CORBIN,
  U. S. Army.

August 20, 1892.
NORMAN S. BRIDGE,
  Los Angeles, Cal.

August 20, 1892.
WALTER S. HAINES,
  Chicago, Ill.

August 21, 1892.
Mrs. WM. POWELL AND CHILDREN,
Misses EVA DUTTON,
  ETTA POWELL,
  DELLA POWELL,
  JENNIE COLTMAN,
  LEONA POWELL,
Mrs. Dr. FRANCIS,
MISS EMMA POWELL,
W. M. FISHER,
CHAS. CLARK,
WM. POWELL,
V. A. POWELL,
HENRY AVERITS,
DEMPSEY POWELL,
  All of Flagstaff, Arizona.

August 23, 1892.
ALFRED AVERYT,
  Shelby, Alabama.

August 23, 1892.
Mrs. R. M. FRANCIS,
  Chillicotho, Missouri.

August 23, 1892.
Miss JENNIE R. COLTMAN,
  Washington, D. C.

August 23, 1892.
Mr. and Mrs. H. F. STEVENS,
  St. Paul, Minn.

August 23, 1892.
Mrs. J. H. HOSKINS,
  Flagstaff, Arizona.

August 23, 1892.
Miss M. E. BECKWITH,
  Baltimore, Md.

August 23, 1892.
C. E. HOWARD,
  Flagstaff, Ariz.

August 25, 1892.
J. J. TAYLOR AND WIFE,
  El Paso, Texas.

Went to the river and back; too tired to write any more.

SCENE ON THE GRAND VIEW TRAIL.

August 27, 1892.
   MARY L. STRIGHT,
      Jemez Hot Springs,
         Archuleta P. O., N. M.

Went to the rock cabin the afternoon of August 25th. The next day went from there to the river and back, and arrived at the rim this morning (August 27th) at half-past ten o'clock.

August 28, 1892.
   ALEX. McDERMID AND WIFE,
      Flagstaff, Arizona.

August 28, 1892.
   J. WOODBRIDGE,
      Flagstaff, Arizona.

August 29, 1892.
   Captain W. HOFFMAN, WIFE, AND CHILD,
      U. S. Army.

September 4, 1892.
   J. W. WILSON,
      Denver, Colo.

September 4, 1892.
   STEPHEN FANCY,
      Aspen, Colo.

September 4, 1892.
   AUGUST REISHEL,
      Turkey.

September 4, 1892.
   SCHUYLER CASE,
      Denver, Colo.

September 7, 1892.
   WM. H. ALLEY AND WIFE,
      Chicago.

Visited Moran Point and Grand View Point; went down Hance Trail to river. All should be visited, if strength and time permits.

September 8, 1892.
   Dr. GEO. H. POWERS,
   Mrs. CORELIA C. POWERS,
   RUTH POWERS,
      San Francisco, Cal.

September 8, 1892.
   Mrs. J. D. HOOKER,
      Los Angeles, Cal.

September 8, 1892.
   JOHN H. HICKS,
      Flagstaff, Arizona.

September 12, 1892.
   Mrs. J. D. DeRUSSY,
   J. DALE DeRUSSY,
      Col. 11th Inf. U. S. Army.
   Mrs. B. F. POPE,
      All of Whipple Barracks, A. T.

September 12, 1892.
   I. G. C. LEE,
      B. V. T. Lieut. Col. U. S. Army.
         Los Angeles, Cal.

The grandeur of the views of this day must surely leave a life-long impression. They repay for all the fatigue. I predict that this cañon will become one of the most noted and visited spots of our country. It should be made a great national park.

September 13, 1892.
   Col. FRANK HULL, Jr.,
                     New York.

   After having visited all the noted places in both Europe and America, I have seen nothing to compare with the sublimity of the Grand Cañon. I should advise all Americans to see the most splendid sight of their own country before going abroad. I spent several days fishing in the cañon, and caught many large salmon. I also looked at several of the rich mines, and found to my utter amazement that they were laden with valuable treasures. It will only be a short time until these mines will be opened up and the ore exported to all parts of the world.

September 15, 1892.
   WM. W. MITCHELL,
   ELLA MITCHELL,
                     Cadillac, Mich.

September, 15, 1892.
   EDWARD F. HOBART,
   MARION C. HOBART,
                     Santa Fe, N. M.

September 15, 1892.
   LEVI DAVIS,
                     Lima, Adams County, Ill.

September 15, 1892.
   WALTER E. HALL, M. D.,
   Mrs. MARY H. HALL,
                     Burlington, N. J.

September 15, 1892.
   JESSIE and CHAS. EVERETTE.

   This cañon is simply immense — too big to look at.

September 25, 1892.
   C. W. WOODIN,
                     Lancaster, Ohio.

September 28, 1892.
   J. C. BROWN,
                     East Saginaw, Mich.

September 28, 1892.
   S. B. HILL,
                     Chicago.

September 30, 1892.
   J. A. LAMPORT,
                     Flagstaff, Arizona.

September 30, 1892.
   C. H. FANCHER,
                     Albuquerque, N. M.

September 30, 1892.
   Mr. and Mrs. E. L. HOLMES,

   The grandest, the greatest, the most wonderful sight in the world. No one can tell the immensity of this grand cañon.

October 3, 1892.
   LOWISE BIGLOW TYLER,
                     North Adams, Mass.

October 15, 1892.

S. W. HIBBEN,
H. CLEMENT,
    Los Angeles, Cal.
D. MITCHELL,
    Flagstaff, Arizona.

We left rim at 8 o'clock A.M., arrived at cabin at 9.45 A.M.; arrived at river, 12:10 P.M.; back to rim, 5:10 P.M. Time for entire trip, nine hours and ten minutes, thus beating the world's record. John Hance will verify

October 15, 1892.

ARTHUR LITTLEJOHN,
    Brooklyn, N. Y.

October 30, 1892.

JOHN H. BOWMAN,
Mrs. J. H. BOWMAN,
    Holbrook, Arizona.

October 30, 1892.

A. E. NETTLETON,
    Syracuse, N. Y.

October 30, 1892.

JAMES W. UPSON,
Mrs. LILLIAN B. UPSON,
    Baldwinsville, N. Y.

This party all went to the river without a guide. They rated it very grand, and all that has been claimed. However, if future parties of camping ladies intend going down, would advise them to employ the guide, and go prepared for roughing it. The ladies should wear very short wide skirts, and have Hance's burros to help them up from the cabin.

November 14, 1892.

W. F. CODY (Buffalo Bill),
GEO. P. EVERHART,
    Chicago, Ill.
JAMES T. WELLS,
    Salt Lake City.
ALLISON NAILOR,
    Washington, D. C.
FRANK D. BALDWIN,
JOHN M. BURKE,
    U. S. Army.
H. S. BOAL,
    North Platte, Neb.
WM. D. DOWD,
    Flagstaff, A. T.
R. H. HASLAM,
    Chicago, Ill.
Piper Heidsieck.
E. C. BRADFORD,
    Denver, Colo.
W. HENRY MACKINNON,
    England.
W. H. BROACH,
    North Platte, Neb.
DANIEL SEEGMILLER,
MERRITT S. INGRAHM,
    Washington, D. C.

Buffalo Bill Expedition to Grand Canon of Colorado.

Universal comment is that it is too sublime for expression, too wonderful to behold, without awe, and beyond all power of mortal description.

November 14, 1892.

   EDWARD B. RUSSELL,
                     Boston, Mass.

November 14, 1892.

   HERBERT EARLSCLIFFE,

Close of the visiting record for the year 1892.

January 25, 1893.

   WM. O. O'NEILL,

God made the cañon, John Hance the trails. Without the other, neither would be complete.

[The above name, Wm. O. O'Neill (better known in Arizona as "Buckey" O'Neill), who has written his name in this private visitors' book, was killed while defending his country, between the hours of 10 and 11 A.M., July 1, 1898, near Santiago de Cuba. He was made Captain of Troop A, 1st U. S. Volunteer Cavalry, and was making ready for the charge on San Juan Hill, Santiago de Cuba, when he was struck by a Mauser bullet and killed.

Captain O'Neill was carried from the front about two hundred yards back from where he fell, on what is known as "Bloody Ford," on San Juan Creek, and buried by Chaplain Brown, Corporal C. C. Jackson (of Flagstaff, Arizona), Privates Robt. Wren, Teddy Burke, and —— Vansicklin.]

January 25, 1893.

   JOHN MARSHALL,
             Good luck for 1893.

Easter Sunday, April 2, 1893.

Trusting you will have an enjoyable season, we are yours truly,—

   JOHN M. WHITMAN,
                     Chicago, Ill.
   HOMER M. WILLIAMS AND WIFE,
   Mrs. E. W. DOWLING,
                     New York.
   DANIEL RUTTER AND WIFE.

P. S.—We are reported the first visitors of the season, and cannot find words to express our admiration and astonishment of the Grand Cañon.

   J. LOGAN SAMPLE,
                     Pittsburg, Pa.

   JAMES A. PITTS,
                     Flagstaff, Arizona.

   M. M. FISHER,
                     Flagstaff, A. T.

   Dr. C. B. PENROSE,
   Mrs. PENROSE,
                     Philadelphia, Pa.

April 17, 1893.

   J. A. OBER AND WIFE,
                     Milford, N. H.

April 18, 1893.
   TOMMIE ASHURST,
           Flagstaff, Arizona.

April 18, 1893.
   Miss CHRISMAN,
           Flagstaff, A. T.

April 20, 1893.
   Miss L. BALLAD,
           Portland, Maine.

April 20, 1893.
   Miss IRENE HUNT,
           Newport, R. I.

   JNO. M. CLARK,
           Flagstaff, Arizona.
Arrived the 18th; left the 21st of April, 1893.

April, 1893.
   Mr. and Mrs. WOLSELEY,
           British Guiana.

April, 1893.
   Dr. and Mrs. HERBERT L. BURRELL,
           Boston, Mass.

April, 1893.
   H. H. RAGAN,
           Syracuse, N. Y.

April, 1893.
   M. G. HEINEY,
           Jacksonville, Ill.

April, 1893.
   J. S. HYDE,
           Titusville, Pa.

April, 1893.
   PAUL C. OSCANYAN,
           New York City.

   JAMES I. MANSON,
           Moqui, Ariz.

April, 1893.
   J. T. HERNDON,
           Franklin, Ky.

May 10, 1893.
   J. W. ARNOTT,
           Beverley, England.
Arrived May 15th; descended into the cañon this day.

May 17, 1893.

B. W. CLOWD,
                Woodbury, N. J.

Arrived May 16th; descended part way into cañon; met Mr. John Hance and Mr. Arnott returning. Ascended with them, and had a pleasant conversation for an hour in Mr. Hance's cottage. Exchanged a five dollar gold piece for an English sovereign at a point where man never before passed money.

May, 1893.

H. H. WATKINS,
                Philadelphia.

May, 1893.

L. WATKINS,
                Chicago.

WM. VERNON BOOTH,
                Chicago, Ill.

WILLIAM B. DOWD,
                New York.

May 18, 1893.

MARSHALL H. MALLORY,
ROLLAND MALLORY,
                New York.

May 20, 1893.

J. W. DOUBLEDAY,
                Jamestown, New York.

May 20, 1893.

C. WALLIS,
                Edgbasten, England.

May 20, 1893.

C. WALLIS.

Having visited the principal points of interest in Europe, as well as in America, I would say that I have seen nothing like the Grand Cañon of the Colorado for grandeur and for its unique views.

May 20, 1893.

J. W. DOUBLEDAY.

Having gone down the cañon to the winter cabin of Mr. Hance, I must say that the cañon changes to the view at every few hundred feet, and the small hillocks that open from the rim change to mountains as you go down.

May 21, 1893.

HUGO LANGEWITZ RIGA,
                Russland, Russia.

June 2, 1893.

HENRY T. FINCK AND WIFE.

Doubtless the most unique sight in the world, and the greatest possible surprise is to walk up from these tents to the edge of the cañon to realize the full depth of the cañon. The visitor should look at it from the rim on the point just this side of Point Bissell. The morning light is best from that position, while from the station the best hours are 4 to 7 P.M.

COLORADO RIVER — LOOKING UP FROM GRAND VIEW TRAIL.

June 8, 1893.

   J. W. FLAVELLE,
London.

   To river and Bissell's Point.

June 11, 1893.

   FREDERICK DIRNBURG,
Berliner Tageblatt,
Berlin, Germany.

   Dr. ERNEST H. VON HALLE,
Hamburg, Germany.

   BERNHARD DERBURG,
Berlin, Germany.

   Dr. PHIL ALWIN VICTOR,
Germany.

   MAX TELIGER,
Berlin, Germany.

   HANS TELIGER,
Berlin, Germany.

   Party of German Editors and Artists.

June 14, 1893.

   J. H. TOLFREE,
   Mrs. J. H. TOLFREE,
Mojave, Cal.

June 17, 1893.

   W. S. BARTLETT,
Santa Ana, Cal.

   The grandeur of the Grand Cañon of the Colorado River rivals, if it does not exceed, that of the Yosemite Valley.

June 18, 1893.

   S. L. COX AND WIFE,
Webb City, Mo.

   C. F. COX,
Carthage, Mo.

   W. J. GREGG AND WIFE,
Flagstaff, Arizona.

   WM. SAWYER,
Flagstaff, Ariz.

   All went to river on the 17th. Spent night at cabin, and returned to rim morning of 18th.

June 27, 1893.

   Rev. SELAH BROWN.

   Left July 1, 1893.

July 1, 1893.

   HERMAN JOHANSSON,
Stockholm, Sweden.

   The greatest sight I have ever seen.

July 4, 1893.

   Mrs. J. H. TOLFREE.

July 4, 1893.

   L. E. CHITTENDEN,
Mojave, Cal.

   Went to the river July 4th; returned July 5th. Had a most glorious time. Will never forget my Fourth of July in the cañon. It is one of the grandest sights in the world.

July 5, 1893

    J. J. SHAUM,
                      1744 Market st.,
                      Philadelphia, Pa.

I fully agree with the above, and desire to register this statement that a pleasant lady adds much to the enjoyment of the trip.

July 5, 1893.

    L. E. CHITTENDEN,
                      Mojave, Cal.

After ascending from the winter cabin this A.M., Mr. Hance returned, leaving the rim at 10:40, and reaching the winter cabin 11:05, making the descent of 3,300 feet — three miles — in twenty-eight minutes. He immediately returned to the rim, arriving at 12:10, being sixty-two minutes for the ascent, and one hour and thirty minutes for the entire trip. Considering the ground over which this six miles extend, it was a wonderful trip. I timed and witnessed the descent and ascent from the rim.

July 5, 1893.

    WM. SATORI,
                      Yankton, Dakota.

July 5, 1893.

    BEN P. HOOKE, Jr.
                      Logsville, Pa.

July 6, 1893.

    GEO. WHITFIELD,
                      Wimbledon, England.

Arrived July 5th; left July 11th. Bathed in the Colorado River July 6th.

July 10, 1893.

    Mr. and Mrs. WM. DOWNS,
                      Brooklyn, New York.

Enjoyed very much the visit. Went down to the river, which, under Hance's lead, is well worth the labor.

July 11, 1893.

    Dr. GUSTAV BRUHL,
                      Cincinnati, Ohio.

July 11, 1893.

    JOS. B. VERCAMP,
    Mrs. JOSEPH B. VERCAMP,
                      Cincinnati, Ohio.

July 11, 1893.

    Mrs. D. BABBITT,
    RAYMOND BABBITT,
                      Flagstaff, Ariz.

July 14, 1893.

    J. A. LEONARD,
                      Youngstown, Ohio.

The Grand Cañon,—a great gulf of pale blue transparent ether in which is submerged unspeakable sublimity and indescribable beauty.

July 14, 1893.
    DIETRICH KREMICRLT,
               Augsburg, Germany.
    C. GRAF BLUCHER,
               Berlin, Germany.
All went to the river.

July 24, 1893.
    EUGENE A. HILL,
               Wichita, Kan.

July 25, 1893.
    MATHIAS YOST,
       Santa Ana, Orange County,
               California.

July 25, 1893.
    F. H. LUNGREEN,
               U. S.

July 25, 1893.
    J. H. HICKS,
               N. M.

July 25, 1893.
    GERTRUDE KETCHUM,
    FRANCIS KETCHUM,
               Chicago, Ill.

July 25, 1893.
    WALLACE FORD,
               Dallas, Texas.

July 25, 1893.
    Mr. and Mrs. FRANK H. SCOTT,
    BERTRAM DELAFIELD SCOTT,
    MARION STURGES SCOTT,
               Chicago, Ill.

C. J. SPELLMIRE,
               Flagstaff, Arizona.

DANIEL DONAVAN,
               Chicago, Ill.

J. E. EDWARDS,
               N. C.

KATHARINE EDWARDS,
               California.

CHAS. EDWARDS,
MAUD M. EDWARDS,
               Santa Ana, Cal.

Mrs. A. H. SPELLMIRE,
               K. C., Mo.

ALPHONSO SPELLMIRE,
               Los Angeles, Cal.

ELEANOR SPELLMIRE,
               Cincinnati, Ohio.

July, 1893.
   JAMES HAUXHURST,
   ELLA E. HAUXHURST,
   ADELE HAUXHURST,
   C. W. SIRCH,
                          Phoenix, A. T.

   Mr. and Mrs. JOHN DAVIS,
                          Camp Verde, Ariz.

   SHARLOT M. HALL,
                          Lynx Creek, Ariz.

July, 1893.
   V. E. MESSINGER,
                          Phoenix, Arizona.

July, 1893.
   ROBERT F. GARNETT,
      Cor. Van Buran and Pinal Sts.,
                          Phoenix, Arizona.

August 2, 1893.
   A. BRUCE,
                          England.

August 2, 1893.
   ARTHUR RICMERSCHIER,
                          Munchen, Bavaria.

August 2, 1893.
   KAREL L. DORDRECHT,
                          Holland.

August 2, 1893.
   A. V. STOLK,
                          Rotterdam.

August 2, 1893.
   G. ELPEN,
                          Munchen, Bavaria.

August 2, 1893.
   C. TAUFKIRCHEN,
                          Munchen, Bavaria.

   Prof. T. SINGER,
                          Vienna, Austria.

   Dr. KARMER,
                          Germany.

   B. BUISSON,
                          France.

   W. M. CLAYPOOL,
                          El Paso, Texas.

J. W. WOOD,
  Los Angeles Times.

Almighty Jove, Thy wondrous hand hath carved with skill this cañon grand.

WM. H. BANKS,
            England.

JOHN H. DAWSON,
            San Francisco, Cal.

J. S. HUTCHISON,
Miss K. T. HUTCHISON,
E. C. HUTCHISON,
            San Francisco, Cal.
LINCOLN HUTCHISON,
JAMES S. HUTCHISON,
            Harvard.

Made to cañon and back in 12 hours.

September, 1893.

MATTISON W. CHASE,
  Ogdensburg, New York.

Nature's masterpiece is what I call the Grand Cañon of the Colorado. Why Americans will go to Europe and around the world, where they can see nothing to equal it, before they have looked upon this marvelous spectacle in their own land, I cannot imagine. On September 12th I made the trip, with guide, from the rim down Hance trail to the river, and returned, in eleven hours; but I would advise any one else of average strength and endurance to take the usual two days for the trip.

L. WATTS AND WIFE,
A. WATTS,
            London.

Had a most enjoyable trip. Mr. Hance is most anxious I should mention the fact that we all went to the river. Slept two nights at the rock cabin.

Mrs. W. A. CLARK,
Mrs. K. L. CLARK,
            New York City.
C. W. CLARK,
            Butte, Montana.

We enjoyed the beautiful scenery from Bissell's Point as well as from the river's banks. It is an enjoyable trip.

O. G. SONECK,
            New York.

Dr. BERVERDAY,
            Hanover, Germany.

October 1, 1893.

Rev. Father ALFRED QUETU,
  Parish Priest.
            Prescott, A. T.

October 1, 1893.

Rev. Father FELIX DILLY,
  Parish Priest,
            Flagstaff, Arizona.

October 1, 1893.
  Rev. THOS. C. MOFFETT,
      Flagstaff, Arizona.

October 1, 1893.
  Hon. E. G. F. HORN,
      Prescott, Arizona.

October 1, 1893.
  M. J. DORAN,
      Flagstaff, Arizona.

October 1, 1893.
  A. H. SPELLIRE,
      Flagstaff, Arizona.

October 2, 1893.
  Mrs. WALLACE,
  WM. WALLACE,
  MARGARET WALLACE,
  LORA BELL WALLACE,
  CORA LOVELL,
  LILLIE LOVELL,
  CLARA CALKINS,
  A. JOHNSTON,
  W. H. ASHURST,
  M. M. ASHURST,
  E. J. ASHURST,
  ANDREW ASHURST,
  CHAS. ASHURST,
      All of Flagstaff, Arizona.

October 4, 1893.
  J. CLAUD BILLINGSLEA,
      Chicago, Ill.

October 4, 1893.
  J. H. MEANS,
      Flagstaff, Arizona.

October 4, 1893.
  IVAN QUILK,
      Budapest, Hungary.

October 4, 1893.
  LORDISLAS DE FOGER,
      Budapest, Hungary.

October 4, 1893.
  BARO B. GASTAS,
      Hungary.

October 4, 1893.
  MIRR BERG,
      Hungary.

October 4, 1893.
  JULIA C. PATTERSON,
      London.

WATER TRAIN — ON GRAND VIEW TRAIL.

October 4, 1893.
CHAS. W. K. LEOSER,
New York.

October 4, 1893.
BYRAN E. WOODCOCK,
Pennsylvania.

October 4, 1893.
CHAS. B. McCOY,
Needles, Cal.

October 10, 1893.
J. EDWARD BLAVEL,
Alameda, Cal.

The World's Fair at Chicago is the greatest wonder of the age. The Grand Cañon of the Colorado the greatest wonder of all ages.

October 10, 1893.
R. W. SCHOPPER,
Zerlenroda, Russia.

October 10, 1893.
JOHN COLSHURN,
Langenberg.

October 26, 1893.
L. de BUYGENON,
Liege, Belgique.

After having visited the Yellowstone Park, seen Oregon State and Washington State, Cascade Range, Mt. Tacoma, Mt. Bather, Mt. Shasta, and Sierra Nevada Mountains, California, and the lovely Yosemite Valley, I declare I did not see in America a scenery more or as strikingly wonderful and impressive and sublime as the Grand Cañon of the Colorado. In Europe, I do not remember I have ever seen anything by which I have been as impressed except, perhaps, by the splendid White Mount at Chamoise, when I saw it for the first time fifteen years ago.

October 31, 1893.
L. H. TOLFREE,
Mrs. L. H. TOLFREE,
EDITH M. TOLFREE,
GERTRUDE TOLFREE,
All of Flagstaff, Ariz.

Departed from cañon October 31, 1893.

November 25, 1893.

Left New York City, November 15th, *en route* to California, but my suspicion of the grandeur of the country compelled me to stop off at Flagstaff. The time of the year for a trip to the cañon was anything but safe, considering the lateness of the year, cold weather, and idea of being snowed in, but, nevertheless, our trip was without events of any mention until the night of our arrival at Captain John Hance's, when a terrific snow-storm set in. It lasted until morning. The wind at the present time is blowing a gale, and how we will find it on our return is a question. Must trust to Providence for a safe return. The kind hospitality shown us by Captain John Hance will never be forgotten. During this writing we are all sitting around the fire. To compare the grandeur of this cañon is beyond my power. I can hardly believe my eyes, and must say every one that goes sightseeing should never forget the Grand Cañon of the Colorado.

   Sincerely yours,

 E. T. PAHMENBERG, New York.

Close of visiting record for year 1893.

April 3, 1894.

 WM. C. WILKINSON,
  Prof. of Poetry.
    University, Chicago.

April 6, 1894.

 THOS. BOYNTON, F. S. A.
  Bridlington Quay, England.

Indescribably grand.

April 8, 1894.

 L. B. HICKOK,
  Troy Grove, La Salle Co., Ill.

Words will not describe the Grand Cañon.

April 8, 1894.

 GEO. W. HANCE,
  Yavapai County, Ariz.

April 24, 1894.

 HERBERT B. TURNER,
 Mrs. HERBERT B. TURNER,
 ANNE TRACY TURNER,
 MARY BEACH TURNER,

April 24, 1894.

 ROSALIE DELAFIELD FLOYD,
  22 Williams St.,
   New York City.

April 24, 1894.

 WALTER H. CRITTENDEN,
  New York City.

D. O. WICKHAM AND WIFE,
  No. 1 Broadway,
   New York.

April 26, 1894.

 HERBERT M. TOLFREE,
  Buffalo, N. Y.

April 26, 1894.

 A. G. HUBBARD AND WIFE,
  Redlands, Cal.

Left May 5, 1894.

May 2, 1894.

 Mrs. EDMON WRIGHT,
 Miss BESSIE WRIGHT,
 JOHN CASTLE WRIGHT.

May 2, 1894.
   GEO. D. B. DARBY,
                Philadelphia, Penn.

May 5, 1894.
   WILLIAM G. DeWITT,
                New York City.

One of the greatest wonders of the cañon is the cliff called "Hance's Leap," not generally known. The mountain-sheep got away and crossed the Colorado. Uncle John will give all details, as he is the sole survivor in these parts.

May 7, 1894.
   Miss GERTIE KETCHUM.

May 7, 1894.
   ROBERT CURTIS.

May 7, 1894.
   EUGENE A. SLIKER.

May 11, 1894.
   JOHN H. TRENT,
                Brooklyn, New York.

May 11, 1894.
   Dr. ELBERT WING,
                Chicago.

May 11, 1894.
   FRANK H. SCOTT,
   BERTRAM SCOTT,
                Chicago.

May 11, 1894.
   Miss ELIZA V. RUMSEY,
                Chicago.

May 11, 1894.
   Miss MARY D. STURGES,
   Miss ROSALIE STURGES,
   GEO. STURGES,
                Chicago.

May 11, 1894.
   W. F. DUMMER,
   Mrs. W. F. DUMMER,
                Chicago.

May 11, 1894.
   F. H. LUNGREEN,
                Cincinnati.

May 11, 1894.
   JOHN H. HICKS,
                Flagstaff, Arizona.

May 11, 1894.
   GERTIE KETCHUM,
                Flagstaff, Arizona.

May 11, 1894.
F. C. REID,
   Flagstaff, Arizona.

May 11, 1894.
STANTON CURTIS,
   Flagstaff, Arizona.

May 11, 1894.
Miss BLANCH METZ,
   Cincinnati.

May 11, 1894.
Miss VERKAMP,
   Cincinnati.

May 11, 1894.
WM. BABBITT,
   Flagstaff, Arizona.

May 11, 1894.
N. A. CAMERON,
   Flagstaff, Arizona.

May 11, 1894.
JOHN TOLER,
   Flagstaff, Arizona.

May 11, 1894.
WALLACE FORD,
   Flagstaff, Arizona.

May 11, 1894.
FRANK KETCHUM,
   Flagstaff, Arizona.

May 11, 1894.
E. A. SLIKER,
   Flagstaff, Arizona.

May 12, 1894.
Mrs. W. H. STEVENS,
MARY M. STEVENS,
   Both of Detroit, Mich.

May 12, 1894.
PERCIVAL HENDERSON,
   El Paso, Texas.

May 12, 1894.
JAMES SUYDAM,
LAMBERT SUYDAM,
JED. FRYE,
   All of New York City.

May, 1894.
CHAS. W. PALMIE.

May, 1894.
HEINRICH VOGEL,
   Dresden, Germany.

June 1, 1894.

    Mrs. SUMNER BABCOCK,
    SUMNER BABCOCK.

Arrived June 1st at Moran's Point; Sunset, June 2d; June 3d, down the Grand Cañon to the river, by the way of Red Cañon and Lauras Gorge. Time from river to rim, three and a half hours. No language can describe the grandeur of the trip. June 5th, *en route* to the Yosemite Valley and Yellowstone Park.

June 4, 1894.

    SAM HUBBARD, Jr.,
        San Francisco, Cal.

Where Alph, the sacred river, ran through
    caverns measureless to man,
Down to a sunless sea,
Take the wild imagination of Coleridge,
Take the wonderful masterpieces of Doré,
Yet, neither poet nor painter has ever conceived this sublime reality.

June 20, 1894.

    C. L. BINGHAM,
        Chicago, Ill.

June 23, 1894.

    J. M. CONNELL,
    Mrs. J. M. CONNELL,
    Master RAYMOND CONNELL,
    FRANCIS CONNELL,
        Chicago.

June 23, 1894.

    Miss EDITH LOCKELT,
        Chicago.

June 23, 1894.

    E. WELLS KILOGG,
        Milwaukee, Wisconsin.

June 23, 1894.

    W. H. PICKERING,
        Cambridge, Mass.

June 23, 1894.

    A. E. DOUGLASS,
        Cambridge, Mass.

June 23, 1894.

    CHAS. G. SLACK,
        Marietta, Ohio.

July 18, 1894.

    B. C. HOCK,
        Flagstaff, Arizona.

July 18, 1894.

    GEO. H. SICREST,
        Phoenix, A. T.

July 18, 1894.
    BERRY J. BOSTWICK,
            Phoenix, A. T.

July 18, 1894.
    J. H. POLITZER,
            Phoenix, A. T.

July 18, 1894.
    J. S. BURTON,
            Phoenix, A. T.

July 18, 1894.
    J. T. SPANGLER,
            Phoenix, A. T.

August 9, 1894.
    P. B. McCABE,
            Phoenix, A. T.

Words are inadequate to describe the sublimity of a sunset view of the Grand Cañon of the Colorado, and should be counted among the Seven Wonders of the world.

September 9, 1894.
    J. DOYLE,
            New York.

September 9, 1894
    C. S. SARGENT,
            Brooklyn, N. Y.

September 9, 1894.
    J. W. TOURMEY,
            Tucson, A. T.

September 15, 1894.
    Mr. and Mrs. D. R. GOUCHER,
            Carthage, Mo.

September 21, 1894.
    Mrs. E. H. CHASE,
            New York City, N. Y.

September 21, 1894.
    Dr. A. I. BOUFFLEUR,
    Miss GRACE F. BOUFFLEUR,
            Chicago.

September 21, 1894.
    C. H. FANCHER,
      Land Agt. A. P. R. R.
    HATTIE W. FANCHER,
    GRACE FANCHER,
    WARD FANCHER,
            Albuq., N. M.

We all went down the new trail on September 21st to the river, starting about 8 A.M., and returned about 7 P.M., riding horseback nearly all the way.

September 28, 1894.
    B. N. FREEMAN,
    Mrs. B. N. FREEMAN,
    Miss HELEN FREEMAN,
            Denver, Colorado.

A RESTING-PLACE—AT HEAD OF GRAND VIEW TRAIL.

September 28, 1894.
  W. O. COLE,
  Miss BLANCH E. COLE,
          Chicago, Ill.

September 28, 1894.
  Miss FORD,
          Boston, Mass.

October 7, 1894.
  S. F. MEGUIRE,
  Mrs. S. F. MEGUIRE,
  ALVIE MEGUIRE,
  Little FRANKIE MEGUIRE,
  WM. G. BAILEY,
  Miss LEOTIA STONE,
          Jerome, Ariz.

Visited Grand Cañon via Hance's new trail.

November 8, 1894.
  D. T. BRAINARD,
    First Lieut. 2d Cavalry, U. S. Army.

November 12, 1894.
  D. K. FITZHUGH,
    Special Examiner Pension Bureau,
          Washington, D. C.

To Grand Cañon and back this day, on foot, and I will never forget it. Went to river, via Hance's New Trail. The grandest sight in the world.

November 16, 1894.
  J. H. STEVENSON.

My only regret is that John Hance and I can't make a longer stop at the boss ditch of the world.

March 19, 1895.
  R. K. WILLIS,
          Lewis Centre, Delaware Co., Ohio.

I wish to say that I have seen a good deal of this great and beautiful land of ours, and calling on the great God that made all these beautiful sights, I wish to say that right here on the ranch owned by John Hance is the greatest sight in the world, and I want all my friends on earth to come and enjoy the sights and his open heart and hospitality.

March 19, 1895.
  NEWTON CHALKER,
          Akron, Ohio.

I have spent two days very pleasantly visiting the Grand Cañon of the Colorado, and enjoying the accommodations at the inn of John Hance, and enjoyed both hugely.

April 18, 1895.
  JAS. N. BETHUNE,
          Los Angeles.

April 18, 1895.

HUGH J. LEE,
E. P. TOBIE, Jr.,
   Pawtucket, R. I.

We, Us and Company went from Hance's cabin to the river and returned in four and a quarter hours.

April 27, 1895.

H. P. SPENCER,
   Denver, Colo.

Simply indescribable.

April 27, 1895.

C. O. HALL,
   Conway, Iowa.

  Editor Journal.

After a two days' visit to the Grand Cañon of the Colorado is all that it is represented to be, and more, too. No language can fully describe, no artist paint the beauty, grandeur, immensity and sublimity of this most wonderful production of Nature's great architect. It must be seen to be appreciated.

April 30, 1895.

W. WEST DURANT,
   New York.

It is presumption to attempt to express in mere words the impression made upon one by the Grand Cañon of the Colorado, even after viewing it more than once. It must be seen to be understood and even in part appreciated.

April 30, 1895.

L. N. STOTT,
   Stottville, N. M.

The only part of the cañon I feel I have seen is Mr. Hance's trail. Any one who does not take the trip down into the cañon misses the grandest part of that little part, which you can see in three days' time.

May 7, 1895.

TILLIE VERKAMP.

May 7, 1895.

CLARA WESSEL.

May 7, 1895.

I. H. W.

Drink Condit and Mercur's Orange Cider.

May 20, 1895.

CLARENCE M. SMITH,
   54 Wall St., N. Y.

The Grand Cañon is simply sublime. A trip should be made down Captain Hance's trail to the river, but the traveler must keep his helm hard-a-port. My personal experience in a jaunt to the river and returning in one day, bids me quote Virgil's description of a visit to Hades, of which he says: *Facilis Averno descensus est; Sed reddere.* (That's the rub.)

May 31, 1895.
Miss WHITLOCK,
Mrs. WHITLOCK.

You may talk of this and that point and view, but give us the Hance Point, with shifting clouds and sun playing at hide-and-seek over Santa Fé Temple.

Grand Cañon, June 5, 1895.
Mrs. MARY E. HART, M. D.,
Los Angeles.

There is a certain malady, commonly termed "big head," with which a large number of otherwise healthy people are afflicted.

Prescription: Stand upon the brink of the Grand Cañon, gaze down, and still further down, into its awful depths, and realize for the first time your own utter insignificance.

June 9, 1895.
W. B. THOMAS,
Los Angeles.

I have seen what is without doubt the grandest natural wonder in the world, the Grand Cañon of the Colorado, and I have also seen enough to convince me that no man or woman should attempt to make the trip to the river a-foot. If you can't go on a horse, don't go.

June 9, 1895.
T. S. VAN DYKE,
Los Angeles, Cal.

All it is said to be, and the trail one of the safest I have ever seen.

June 11, 1895.
J. H. TOLFREE,

If the mountains of the earth were leveled off and dumped into the Grand Cañon of the Colorado at this point, there would not be a trail wide enough for a thoroughbred Indian to cross upon.

June 12, 1895.
TESSA L. KELSO,

A better thing than writing in John Hance's book is riding down John Hance's trail to the river.

June 14, 1895.
RUE H. HARDENBERG,

Magnificent, and much else also in addition besides.

June 14, 1895.
ALFRED P. GRIFFITH,
Azusa, Cal.

The grandest sight of my life, and far above possible anticipation, but Captain Hance's double-breasted tea can't be surpassed.

June 14, 1895.
EFFIE B. GRIFFITH,
Rushville, Ill.

My first horseback ride or any stage. I took the cañon trip on Captain Hance's horse Dick, and am alive to tell the tale. I can never forget what I have seen.

Grand Cañon, June 16, 1895.

HARRY T. CORY, C. E.,
Columbia, Mo.

Yesterday I went with Captain Hance to the river. It certainly was the experience of my life. One really has never seen the cañon until he has gone down the trail to the river. After that trip he will certainly agree with me that the cañon is the most awful, horrible thing ever conceived of, and for heaven's sake don't go alone nor walk. To save money by walking, or going alone, is the worst way of saving money I can conceive of. If you do save money (falsely, so called,) just read this when you get back, and remember that I told you so.

July 17, 1895.

JOHN W. SEARGEANT,
Mrs. W. F. SEARGEANT AND CHILDREN,
Marshall, Mo.

July 25, 1895.

ED. B. CULLINAM,
372 W. Seventh, St.
Cincinnati, O.

EZRA J. WARNER, Jr.,
Chicago, Ill.

JOSEPH E. Z. HUNT,
Honolulu,
Hawaiian Islands.

JOHN HUNTER STEARNS,
Chicago, Ill.

July 29, 1895.

H. H. PRUGH,
CARRIE M. PRUGH,
Dayton, Ohio.

This is our fourth day here. Have been down the new trail with John Hance, and made various excursions along the rim. We feel that we have only commenced to realize the unspeakable sublimity of the cañon, and hope to come again when the railroad is built from Flagstaff.

July 31, 1895.

ALDACE F. WALKER,
KATHARINE WALKER,
S. F. GILBERT,
ROBERT WALKER,
HAROLD WALKER,
All of Chicago.

August 1, 1895.

L. W. JOHNSON,
GEO. BURGESS,
W. E. GRAVES,
CHAS. BURKHART,
G. A. McCLAFLIN,
R. S. McCLAFLIN,
J. G. AXLING,
Mrs. R. S. McCLAFLIN,
Mrs. GEO. IRWIN,
Miss ORA RUFFCORN,

Miss ANNIE STUMP,
Miss LYDIA MORRIS,
Miss MAGGIE TYNAN,
                  Winslow, A. T.

August 1, 1895.
CHAS E. BURKHART.
Cooked for the Winslow party.

Grand Cañon, August 19, 1895.
G. A. NEEFF.

We have enjoyed everything,— the faces, the characters, the meals, this book; last, but not least, ah! the cañon. We have seen its faces,— oh, so varied, somber, smiling, meditatingly, growling, ecstatic. To have seen the faces of the mountains and the depths is to have studied the thousand characters, and yet but to catch an inkling of its true worth. It is a book, this cañon is, to the poetic soul, and with such convivial spirit about these venerable trees and kind, smiling faces at the camp, it is one of the most restful places imaginable. The cañon itself is a picture of eternal rest. May the time soon come when many will enjoy the beauties of these God-given festivities.

August 21, 1895.
CHAS. A. BALEY,
                  Oakland, Cal.
WM. C. VAUGHAN,
                  Chicago, Ill.

We made this day the ascent of Ayer's Peak. A flag was placed on the northern peak, one on the southern, and a monument reared on the middle one. Ayer's Peak occupies a central position in the Grand Cañon, from which are revealed such a touch of immensity and grandeur as to produce an indelible impression.

August 22, 1895.
CAROLINE HADLEY
(Aged nine years).

We have been to Moran Point, and we would like to go to the river, but I do not think we can. I think it is very, very deep, and grand, and that it must have taken a very long time to make it. I would like to stay here forever, it is so beautiful.

Grand Cañon, August 25, 1895.
C. H. COBLE,
L. L. FERRAL,
T. B. BELL,
F. D. MYERS,
J. M. AITKEN.
            Bicycle party.

Bell, Myers and Aitken made the trip over the Hance trail on foot. Time, from head of trail to river, two hours and twenty-five minutes; rested two hours, and made the head of the trail in four hours and fifteen minutes.

August 30, 1895.
I. T. WHITTEMORE,
                  Florence, Arizona.

The longings of my heart have been gratified. My anticipations and expectations more than realized. I look in wonder, love, and admiration at this mightiest of God's created works, but never have I felt so small, and God so great, as while standing, awe-struck and overwhelmed, as in gazing on this, the greatest of all earthly wonders. I cannot leave, however, without leaving my testimony of respect for the man who made the trail, and made it possible for all sight-seers to see the cañon from crest to base. All honor to friend John Hance.

Grand Cañon, August 31, 1895.
EDITH MANSFIELD.

Doubtless, God might have made something more wonderful or more magnificent, but, doubtless, he never did. America for Americans. I am glad to add my meed, respect, and admiration for the enterprise and determination which made the trail possible.

August 31, 1895.
MARIAN SCOTT FRANKLIN.

A vision of what God has prepared for us in the New Jerusalem.

August 31, 1895.
HOWARD MARINE,
Flagstaff, Arizona.

Views from Moran's and Bissell's Points are the finest you will see, and go down the trail, and you will know the depth of the cañon by experience.

August 31, 1895.
Miss MAYBEL MYERS,
Phoenix, Arizona.

August 31, 1895.
Miss MARY SMITH,
Phoenix, A. T.

August 31, 1895.
JOHN Y. T. SMITH.
Phoenix, Arizona.

To Mr. John Hance:—

My Old Friend: I am delighted to meet you on the rim of the Grand Cañon of the Colorado River, after a score or more of years since our last meeting.

August 31, 1895.
Miss WINIFRED SMITH,
Phoenix, A. T.

August 31, 1895.
EDWIN E. CARROLL,
Lawrence, Kan.

September 19, 1895.
R. F. GOBLE,
B. D. GOBLE,
O. K. CUSHING.

The cañon is here to show for itself, and Captain Hance will show it to you.

A COMMODIOUS TENT, GRAND CAÑON.

INTERIOR OF SAME.

September, 19, 1895.
>   Dr. ARTHUR KORN,
>   Munich, Germany.

September 20, 1895.
>   Mrs. J. M. AITKIN,
>   J. A. EVERTS,
>   Q. A. DUTCHER,
>   E. W. DUTCHER, M. D.
>   All of Whipple Barracks, Arizona.
>
>   Beautiful Grand Cañon.

September 20, 1895.
>   HUGO FROMHOLZ,
>   Berlin, Germany.
>
>   Visited the cañon, went only half way down the trail, but was fully satisfied of that. Point Moran pleased me best.

September 25, 1895.
>   W. E. PEDRICK,
>   Denver, Colo.
>
>   On the trail to the river, about half an hour's march from a point opposite Point Moran to the right of the trail among cedars, and about one hundred yards distant from the trail, rises a projecting rock, upon whose side I noticed to-day what appeared from the trail upon the face of the rock to be some kind of reptile, coiled in circles, over a space about four feet long. I had no time to visit it to-day, and hope some geological student will make a close examination, and hope a classification may be arrived at.

September 26, 1895.
>   Dr. G. SOHWATHE,
>   Germany.

September 27, 1895.
>   WM. MARTIA AIKEN,
>   Supervising Architect,
>   Treasury Department,
>   Washington, D. C.

October 1, 1895.
>   FRED J. MADDEN,
>   Clinton, Iowa.
>   EDITH M. TOLFREE,
>   GERTRUDE TOLFREE,
>   Flagstaff, Arizona.
>   PORTER FLEMING,
>   Phoenix, A. T.
>   CHAS. S. FLEMMING,
>   Stanford University.
>
>   Grand Cañon survey party.
>
>   We all expect to see the Grand Cañon from the windows of a palace-car next year. "Dude," the jack-rabbit police-dog, kept us in game.

October 1, 1895.
>   WILL B. HUNTER,
>   Chicago.
>
>   Wonderful cañon,
>   Child of the seas,
>   No man knows thy history,
>   None can solve thy mystery;
>   God-given glimpse of eternity
>   To weak humanity.

October 7, 1895.

Dr. P. G. CORNISH,
        Flagstaff, Arizona.
F. H. NEWMAN,
W. B. HUNTER,
W. F. TALIAFERRO,
        Albuquerque, N. M.
E. A. SLIKER,
        Flagstaff, Arizona.
Captain C. E. HOWARD

Cycling party.

October 7, 1895.

The Arizona Mission Conference of the M. E. Church, by arrangements of Rev. B. M. Danforth, Pastor of the M. E. Church at Flagstaff, visited the Grand Cañon. All agreed that the trip was the event of a lifetime. The party was composed of the following persons:—

Bishop HENRY W. WARREN,
        Denver, Colo.
G. F. BOVARD,
    Supt. Arizona Mission,
        Los Angeles, Cal.
C. J. CHASE AND WIFE,
        Pastor at Phoenix, A. T.
G. F. PIERENAUD,
        Pastor at Prescott, A. T.
ED. DEARBORN AND WIFE,
        Pastor at Alhambra, A. T.
DAVID ROBERTS,
        Pastor Tombstone, A. T.
B. M. DANFORTH,
        Pastor Flagstaff, A. T.
Mrs. HUNT,
        Glendale, Arizona.

The Misses AMY and DAISY DANFORTH,
WILL DANFORTH,
    Family of the pastor at Flagstaff.

We all agree that the Grand Cañon is the greatest thing on earth of its kind, and heartily endorse the entire management, including the Grand Cañon Stage Company, the hotel management, and will not soon forget our guide, Captain John Hance.

Friday, October 25, 1895.

CHAS. P. BOND,
        Boston, Mass., and
        Waltham, Mass.

A single day has given me only a glimpse of this marvelous creation of Nature. That glimpse has, however, been a revelation to me. I have seen all the wonders of the New World that command the admiration of man, but I regard this Grand Cañon of the Colorado River as the grandest of them all. One of God's masterpieces,—its grandeur, its marvelous groupings of Nature's pinnacles, and its vast extent,—is beyond the grasp of human intellect to comprehend, and beyond the power of human language to accurately picture. No pen or pencil can portray its awful grandeur. It is a kaleidoscope of Nature's greatest beauties, furnishing new surprises and new wonders from every point of view. It well deserves a place in the galaxy of the great wonders of the world; climate, country, people, and surroundings, all combine, to make this Grand Cañon of the Colorado River one of the ideal spots on the American Continent. A place where one must always love to come, and from which he goes with much reluctance. It is a place where man must feel, if he never felt it before, the existence of a Creator, in whose presence he is as nothing, and whose ways are past understanding.

Beginning of the season, April 1896.

April 15, 1896.

**E. A. SLIKER,
C. H. COBLE,**
    Flagstaff, Arizona.

The Coconino Cycling Club.

The first cyclers of the season. We all expect to see the cañon from the seat of a flat or hand-car next year.

    Lovingly yours,
      E. A. SLIKER.

April 23, 1896.

Mr. and Mrs. W. D. ELLIS,
    New York City, N. Y.

April 29, 1896.

HARRY FIRVE,
    Albuquerque, N. M.

I have been here two days, and never had so much fun since I had the measles.

May 12, 1896.

J. M. CASSIN,
    Santa Rosa, Cal.

If to see the Grand Cañon for a day or two is so great a pleasure, what must it be to view it daily for years? John Hance alone can tell.

May 12, 1896.

ARTHUR L. SHOLL,
  General Office, P. R. R.,
    Philadelphia, Pa.

I made the trip over the new trail between the hours of 8 A.M. and 5 P.M., spending an hour at the river. The most magnificent walk of my life; but I wish to say to others who may wish to walk, take our respected friend's advice,—a word to the wise is sufficient.

May 12, 1896.

Dr. S. A. KNOPF.

To Mr. Hance I wish a few gold-mines and many years of health and happiness besides.

June 19, 1896.—9 p. m.

CHAS. WM. SIRCH,
    Milwaukee, Wis.

Left morning 23d of June 1896.

    IMPRESSION I.

After the drive, a view,
 A sight of the Cañon grandé,
Regrets of the wearisome drive
 To this corner of the land;—
The scene I admit is rugged,
 But should I seek the course,
When around me are beautiful mountains,
 Already I feel remorse,

'T is not half so big as I expected.
  Oh thoroughly I despise
The travelers who exaggerate,
  Especially as to size.

IMPRESSION II.

A supper, well-served and hot,
  Quite cures a man of the blues,
A sleep in a cool, sweet cot
  Full many regrets subdues.
A breakfast, two burros, a guide,
  A descent from the cañon's rim,
I cared not to explore the cañon,
  But just to be company to him,
My friend, the Professor, from Kansas.
  Afoot I descend the trail.

IMPRESSION III.

At eight we are found well-started;
  At ten we did not fail
To drink at the old stone cabin;
  At eleven the ladders descend;
At twelve we have reached the river,
  Down at the cañon's end.

IMPRESSION IV.

A rest and a plunge in the river,
  And experience in quicksand.
We felt of the current in places,
  'T would most take off one's hand;
At three we prepared for the ascent;
  Scaled falls by ladders and ropes;
I had walked seven miles to the river,
  But returning was most beyond hopes.

IMPRESSION V.

I can solve most difficult problems
  Theorems obscure can pass,
But I frankly acknowledge in high arts
  Is vastly superior the ass.

IMPRESSION VI.

On I struggled, e'er seeking the higher;
  Anon I stopped in fright.
An inch to the left, an inch to the right,
  And this page I 'd not indite.
To appreciate, Oh traveler,
  This cañon's awful height,
You must ascend without burro,
  With your own strong brawn and might;
For where there is no unit of measure
  To calculate the size,
To man the extent of the labor
  Will atone for the failure of eyes.

IMPRESSION VII.

"Carpe diem," and do not fail
  To visit Moran's view,
For though quite weary grows the trail,
  The grandeur will ne'er be forgotten by
    you.

IMPRESSION VIII.

Beautiful was the trip we made
  Down Cameron's trail and through the
    caves.
Impressions of stratas and stalagmites
  will cling to my memory, and more
    I crave.

June 19, 1896.

J. CURTIS WASSON, A. B.
Flagstaff, Arizona.

Came to Grand Cañon Hotel; got out of stage; walked over to rim of cañon; looked out, and Oh!!! June 20th, went down Hance's trail to river, took a bath in river, and returned. June 21st, went to Moran's Point. June 22d, went down Cameron's trail; visited mines, and explored three caves.

Chasm of the Creator,
  Handiwork of His hand,
And of His works none greater
  Is found in all the land.

Great, massive, awful abyss,
   Delving Pluto's artifice,
To keep his realm obscure within,
   From upper worlds of wayward men.

And to our host and hostess kind,
   And daughters fairest of mankind,
Who added to our joy,
   We, friend Sirch and I
Now say good-by,
   And hail our stage, ahoy!

May heaven's pleasure,
   Without measure,
E'er your way betide,
   That others coming,
In the gloaming,
   May e'er in you confide.

August 12, 1896.

  S. SOPHIA FRIEDLEY,
            Morristown, Pa.

August 12, 1896.

  MARY C. STINSON,
            Morristown, Pa.

August 12, 1896.

  GERTRUDE HENDERSON,
            Montgomery, Pa.

August 12, 1896.

  KATHARINE P. FRANCISCENS,
            Lewistown, Pa.

August 12, 1896.

  ROBERT P. SHICK,
            Reading, Pa.

August 12, 1896.

  WM. H. BEAN,
            First Lieut., Second Cavalry, U. S. A.

August 12, 1896.

  WM. STOWE DERVOL,
            University of Arizona,
                 Tucson, Arizona.

It is a chasm to afford a place wherein the soul may seek repose, and which may prompt the deepest emotions to great activity, and lift man above himself.

September 3, 1896.

  Rev. ULYSSES G. B. PIERCE,
            Pomona, Cal.

September 3, 1896.

  Mrs. WM. F. LEWIS,
            Fort Apache, A. T.

September 14, 1896.

  HELEN A. RIORDAN,
            Flagstaff, Arizona.

September 22, 1896.
   V. H. EDMUNDSON, M. D.
                  Gallup, N. M.

September 22, 1896.
   HARRIETTE F. CODWISE,
                  Kingston, N. Y.

September 22, 1896.
   Maj. and Mrs. W. M. WALLACE.

September 30, 1896.
   I. W. RAND,
      First Lieut. Asst. Surgeon, U. S. A.
                  Fort Apache, A. T.

October 23, 1896.
   WM. AUGUST BARROIS,
                  Lile, France.

October 23, 1896.
   L. BERKER.

October 30, 1896.
   KATHARINE ARMS,
   Mrs. CHAS. D. ARMS,
   CAROLYN WICK ARMS,
                  Youngstown, Ohio.

November 15, 1896.
   GEO. E. WHITE,
   MINNIE A. WHITE,
                  Prescott, Arizona.

November 15, 1896.
   N. O. MURPHY,
   NELLIE MURPHY,
                  Prescott, Arizona.

November 28, 1896.
   HERMAN KOBBE,

   Good luck to Captain Hance on his prospecting tour, and may he strike a bonanza.

November 28, 1896.
   MAGNUS C. MYER,
                  Chicago, Ill.

   Many a land has seen my eyes, many a mountain crossed my foot, but never seen such wonderful creations as this,— the Grand Cañon of the Colorado.

Close of the visiting record for the year 1896.

Monday, April 19, 1897.
   The Opening of the Season.
   JAMES G. DUNCAN,
                  Mt. Vernon, N. Y.
   Miss A. ENDICOTT,
                  Martin, N. Y.

CHIMNEY ROCK, GRAND CAÑON.

J. ALEXANDER MOONE, M. D.,
    Helena, Montana.

We all visited Moran and Bissell's Point. A grand sight.

April 24, 1897.

RUDOLF FBACH,
    Barmen, Germany.

April 26, 1897.

P. C. BICKNELL,
    Phoenix, Arizona.

May 1, 1897.

Mr. and Mrs. W. H. WOOLWORTH.
    Niagara Falls, N. Y.

Visited Moran's Point, Bissell's Point, and walked part way down John Hance's trail. Language seems weak and inadequate to the task of describing the grandeur of the Grand Cañon of the Colorado River.

May 5, 1897.

Rev. ULYSSES G. B. PIERCE,
    First Unitarian Church.
FLORENCE LONSBURY PIERCE,
    Pomona, Cal.

Log Hotel dedicated August 6, 1896.

May 5, 1897.

JAMES PRINGLE,
    Edinburgh, Scotland.

Since leaving my native land of Scotland I have traveled upwards of thirty thousand miles,—over three fourths of this globe,—but have nowhere seen so awe-inspiring a sight as the Grand Cañon of the Colorado River, said to be unequaled in the world. I believe no artist has yet been born who can adequately portray it, nor any word-painter can do justice to so majestic a theme. It is, to my mind, a humbling sight, and the main lesson it teaches us is the littleness of man. What is man, that thou art mindful of him?

May 5, 1897.

Miss JONES,
E. A. JONES,
    Both of Brooklyn, N. Y.

May 13, 1897.

F. W. MORRIS, Jr.,
    Philadelphia, Pa.

May 13, 1897.

GEO. S. GERHARD, M. D.
    Philadelphia, Pa.

May 14, 1897.

R. S. HAYES,
ANN N. HAYES,
    Both of New York.

The biggest thing on earth.

May 14, 1897.
   CORLEIA R. BEAN,
   BLANCH BEAN.

Long live the cañon. May its grandeur never grow less.

   ALDACE F. WALKER.
   A. T. & S. F. R. R.
   Endorsement guaranteed.

May 14, 1897.
   HENRY J. CAMGAN,
   Brooklyn, N. Y.

May 16, 1897.
   Mr. and Mrs. THOS. GOFFERY,
   Liverpool.

Went down the cañon, under the guidance of Captain John Hance, and would advise every one else to do likewise, as no proper conception of the cañon can be gained from above.

May 19, 1897.
   W. E. NELSON,
   Quincy, Ill.

May 20, 1897.
   ARTHUR DIXON,
   Illinois.

May 21, 1897.
   Mrs. E. L. REYNOLDS,
   South Bend, Ind.

What are the pyramids of Egypt, works of man, compared to the works of the Almighty.

May 22, 1897.
   AGNES FARRAND,
   South Bend, Ind.

May 22, 1897.
   CATHARINE C. E. SMAY,
   South Bend, Ind.

May 22, 1897.
   EDWARD EVERTT SER,
   Montgomery City, Mo.

In testimony of Captain Hance's idea of truth.

May 22, 1897.
   Dr. MONS CARL MÜLLER,
   Prag, Austria.

   RUDOLF de HALEN,
   Hanover, Germany.

May 24, 1897.

JAMES H. McCLINTOCK,
Phœnix, Arizona.

In his way, Hance is as great as the cañon.

May 25, 1897.

JOHN A. BECKWITH,
Oakland, Cal.

If Dickens had only been John Hance, what a book he could have written. As for the cañon, it is undoubtedly the most wonderful thing of its kind on this earth. The crater of Kilauea, in violent action, is possibly the more impressive of the two.

May 27, 1897.

PREBIN A. LAURING.

May 28, 1897.

GEO. W. REEVE,
ARCHIE REEVE,
Montreal.

May 28, 1897.

JOHN ADAMS LOWELL,
Boston, Mass.

May 28, 1897.

L. MACDONALD,
Montreal, Canada.

May 31, 1897.

KANSAS TOURISTS.

We hope when next
  We visit the cañons,
To find John and
. Peck dearer companions.

May she put on a dress,
  To cover her pants,
And change her name
  To Mrs. John Hance.

May they be supplied
  With plenty of bedding,
When we all come to dance,
  At the Hance-Peck wedding.

John, if ever inclined
  To go on a tipple,
Just go to the cañon,
  And behold Peck's nipple.

May 31, 1897.

J. P. CAMPBELL,
Ashland, Kans.

Next to the Grand Cañon, Captain John Hance and his trail are two of the greatest wonders of the world. The half was never told.

June 1, 1897.

ROBERT W. PARK,
Stockyards,
Kansas City, Mo.

June 1, 1897.

F. MOULTON BARRETT,
    Devon, England.

During our stay at the Grand Cañon, we were much indebted to Captain Hance for his excellent arrangements, courtesy, and his wonderful information.

June 1, 1897.

GILBERT DAVIDSON,
    Devon, England.

I heartily endorse all my friend has said.

June 1, 1897.

M. C. CAMPBELL,
    Wichita, Kans.

El Cañon Grandé de la Colorado is, in my judgment, one of the greatest wonders of the world. Captain Hance, the modern path-finder, well deserving the title.

June 1, 1897.

H. RIEDMAN,
    Hamburg, Germany.

Heartily endorsing everything said above.

June 1, 1897.

JOS. TANGERNAN,
    Newport, Ky.

June 1, 1897.

G. W. MEAD, Jr.,
    Brooklyn, N. Y.

June 6, 1897.

Mr. and Mrs. ERNEST de SASSEVILLE,
    Denver, Colo.

June 10, 1897.

FRANK J. HAHN,
    Philadelphia, Pa.

The kindness of Captain Hance and Mr. Clayton have made our stay a very pleasant one.

June 10, 1897.

EMILIE F. HAHN.

In testimony of the courtesy and kindness of Captain John Hance and Mr. Clayton.

June 11, 1897.

R. W. DANA.

Delighted with everything, even the mules.

June 13, 1897.

CHAS. STANFORD.

Vastly pleased with the whole trip.

June 13, 1897.

P. E. KIPP.

Marvelous are Thy works, and that my soul knoweth right well.

June 18, 1897.

WALTER G. BENTLEY,
200 Randolph St.,
Chicago, Ill.

While memory holds a seat in this distracted orb shall I forget the impression made by this short acquaintance with the greatest of all natural wonders. It is a great pleasure to be able to vouch for Captain John Hance, as guide and friend, without whom tourists would be deprived of the most impressive part of their visit, a trip down the trail to the river. After a trip down the trail and back yesterday, and a visit to Points Moran and Bissell to-day, under the Hance guidance, would certainly urge every visitor to avail himself of Mr. Hance's trail, thereby assuring to himself the very best condition for getting the most value out of his visit.

June 23, 1897.

IRA D. HAVEN, WIFE and DAUGHTER,
Oakland, Cal.

June 26, 1897.

Mr. and Mrs. JOHN R. VOSKAMP,
Pittsburg, Pa.

June 14 to July 1, 1897.

AMELIA B. HOLLENBACK,
Brooklyn, N. Y.

Thank Captain Hance and the cañon for the happiest two weeks any one ever spent.

June 14 to July 1, 1897.

JOSEPHINE W. HOLLENBACK,
Brooklyn, N. Y.

Our expectations for years have been fully and more than happily realized during the last two weeks. To Captain John Hance we are deeply indebted for his untiring courtesy and kindness, which have helped to make our visit at the Grand Cañon all that it has been to us.

July 2, 1897.

**THOS. R. LATTA,
WM. JACK LATTA,
MAMIE LESH LATTA,**
Goshen, Ind.

July 2, 1897.

Mrs. MARY E. LESH,
Goshen, Ind.

July 2, 1897.

Mr. and Mrs. J. A. TAYLOR,
Arrowsmith, Ill.

Words are inadequate to express the awful sublimity and grandeur of the Grand Cañon. Many thanks to Captain John Hance for his kindness.

July 2, 1897.

H. C. McCLURE AND WIFE,
                  Gileson City, Ill.

Whilst life lasts we can never forget the generous kindness and humane hospitality of our friend, Captain John Hance. May he have long life in his well-doing.

July 2, 1897.

T. C. POLING,
                            Quincy, Ill.

Any one who comes to the Grand Cañon, and fails to meet Captain John Hance, will miss half the show. I can certify that he can tell the truth, though it is claimed by his friends that he is not exactly like the Rev. Geo. W. in that particular, as he can do the other thing when necessary to make a story sound right. Long live Captain Hance.

July 7, 1897.

W. A. HALL,
                      Whitewater, Wis.

For the Lord is a Great God. In His hand are the deep places of the earth.—Psalms, xcv:3, 4.

July 7, 1897.

Mr. and Mrs. F. A. PATTEE,
                  Los Angeles, Cal.

Had an out-of-sight time. Words fail to express our delight and satisfaction with all we have seen.

July 7, 1897.

F. A. PATTEE.

My Dear Captain:—

You may build trails into it, up it, and around it; you may ever take a few more of those celebrated horseback-jumps over its crest, but you can never catch up with it. Yours, in the world where they lie still some day.

July 10, 1897.

**LEE DOYLE,
CHESTER BLACK,
JOHNIE DOYLE,
GEORGE BLACK,
JIMMIE SMITH,
BURT DOYLE,**
            All of Flagstaff, Ariz.

July 15, 1897.

S. G. BAYNE,
                          New York.

July 16, 1897.

Dr. B. WALLA,
                Budapest, Hungary.

July 16, 1897.

KALMOIN SAXLETMER,
                Budapest, Hungary.

SCENE FROM HOTEL POINT, GRAND CAÑON.

July 24, 1897.
WM. J. McCLURE,
Stapleton, N. Y.

Traversed the rim of the Grand Cañon of the Colorado River July 24, 1897, and descended to the Colorado River, in company with C. E. Shaver and Captain John Hance, the guide, July 25th. We had, therefore, the double pleasure of a downward and upward view of the glorious Grand Cañon.

July 24, 1897.
C. E. SHAVER,
Phoenix, A. T.

To the river and back from the hotel in eight hours, in company with Father McClure and Captain John Hance.

July 29, 1897.
Mrs. LEAH D. SCANDRETT.

Spent the 30th on the rim near hotel. August 1st, went to Moran's Point. Viewed from any place on the rim, and especially Moran's Point, the cañon is the most sublime and awe-inspiring sight one may ever hope to see on this earth.

July 29, 1897.
H. V. SCANDRETT,
Spearville, Kan.

There are few subjects too large for a Kansasan to tackle, but to express myself on this wonderful masterpiece is to me the exception that proves the rule. Am afraid I shall not be able to tell my friends anything about it, without endangering my standing for truthfulness.

August 7, 1897.
DAVID W. FAHS.

Great and marvelous are Thy works, O Lord. In wisdom hast Thou made them all.

August 10, 1897.
THOS. G. FROST AND WIFE,
Minneapolis.

August 11, 1897.
G. W. PURSELL,
Los Angeles, Cal.

To-day, in company with Captain John Hance, I discovered and explored the first great prominences beyond Fort Hollenbeck, and named the same "Point Diewaido."

August 11, 1897.
RUBY E. COBB,
Denver, Colo.

JAS. S. NIES,
Brooklyn, N. Y.

Full many a song and dance I 've heard,
  Upon the vaudeville stage,
But none can beat the yarns you 'll get
  From Capt. John Hance, I wage.

The woman fat, between the rocks,
  By giant-powder saved
The mare who jumped two thousand feet,
  And other dangers braved.

But to appreciate him best,
Just hear him for yourself,
And let him guide you o'er the trail,
And don't you spare yourself.

August 18, 1897.
   Mrs. ROBERT MURRAY,
              London, Ontario.

August 19, 1897.
   MAGGIE J. MURRAY,
              London, Ontario.

August 19, 1897.
   Dr. W. FREUVENTHAL,
              New York City, N. Y.

August 19, 1897.
   Mrs. D. J. BRANNEN,
              Flagstaff, Arizona.

   The sublimity of the scene forbids all other thoughts except those of reverence and awe.

August 27, 1897.
   C. J. BABBITT,
              Flagstaff, Arizona.

August 27, 1897.
   PAUL H. VERKAMP,
              Cincinnati, Ohio.

August 27, 1897.
   Mrs. ROBERT C. MORRIS,
   ROBERT C. MORRIS,
              Both of New York City, N. Y.

August 27, 1897.
   D. L. E. BRAINARD,
              Captain C. S., U. S. A.

August 29, 1897.
   Dr. T. F. ALLEN,
              New York City, N. Y.

August 29, 1897.
   Miss EVELYN H. NORDHOFF,
              New York City, N. Y.

August 29, 1897.
   Mrs. CHAS. NORDHOFF,
              Coronado Beach, Cal.

August 29, 1897.
   AARON GOLDBURG,
   Miss A. GOLDBURG,
              Both of Phoenix, A. T.

September 14, 1897.
   Mme. ROUNSEVILLE,
              Chicago, Ill.

September 14, 1897.

MARGUERITE SHONTS.

Pleased with everything, even Captain John Hance.

~~~~~~~~~~

September 16, 1897.

A. REICLING,
        San Francisco, Cal.

~~~~~~~~~~

September 25, 1897.

E. W. BOYD,
        Pittsburg, Pa.

Persons visiting the Grand Cañon, without taking the trail to the river, have failed to see the beauty of the place. The trail is perfectly safe. I rode from top to bottom. Enjoyed it hugely. As to John Hance, he is very gentlemanly, but a curiosity of the rarest type.

~~~~~~~~~~

September 26, 1897.

J. F. JACKSON,
        Milwaukee, Wis.

The cañon is all right.

~~~~~~~~~~

September 29, 1897.

J. D. CROISSANT,
        Washington, D. C.

I cheerfully record my name in this book as among those who fully appreciate the grandeur of this great cañon. I have stood upon the brink, and looked down into the mouth of seething Vesuvius; have looked down upon Switzerland's charming lakes from Regi; have climbed to the top of Mt. Washington and Pike's Peak, and have just come from a week's stay in charming Yosemite, and I freely record my opinion that there is nothing on earth that will ever compete with this Grand Cañon. Captain John Hance, our faithful guide, is quite as unique in his way as the cañon itself.

~~~~~~~~~~

September 29, 1897.

DEWITT CLINTON CROISSANT,
        Washington, D. C.

Everything surpasses what it has been cracked up to be; only be sure when ordering a lunch to have them put in an extra sandwich. Captain Hance, with all his lies, is a most trustworthy individual.

~~~~~~~~~~

September 29, 1897.

DAVID FORBES,
        New York City, N. Y.

Glorious, laborious. Glad I went. Thankful it's over. Special thanks to Captain Hance. Splendid guide, in spite of his economy of the truth.

~~~~~~~~~~

September 29, 1897.

GUY L. FRAZER,
        Highlands, Cal.

~~~~~~~~~~

September 29, 1897.

J. A. HOLMES,
    U. S. Geological Survey.
        Chapel Hill, N. C.

October 6, 1897.

    H. CARPENTER,
                    Chicago, Ill.

October 12, 1897.

    ANNIE J. GARLIDE.

Oh my! Oh my! Oh my! The half was never told. Good luck to Captain Hance and all the good people at the Grand Cañon Hotel.

October 16, 1897.

    Mr. and Mrs. J. L. MOSS.

John Hance is half and the Grand Cañon is the other half.

    ANNA M. FLEMING,
    F. S. HAFFORD,
    MARY L. WHITE,
    MARY McGILL,
    STANLY WINDES,
    C. RUTH OPDYKE,
                      Prescott, A. T.

She strode along with a manly stroke,
Till the puckering string of her bloomers broke.

October 23, 1897.

    MABEL A. GARLAND,
                    Pomona, Cal.

October 24, 1897.

    A. JUDSON BALL,
    MARY H. BALL,
                  Mt. Vernon, Ohio.

The half never has been nor never can be told.

THE CAÑON.

Born in an earthquake's shock,
    And carved by the roaring flood,
Ye mighty piles of rock,
    Great handiwork of God.

November 4, 1897.

    F. M. LIVERMORE,
    Mrs. F. M. LIVERMORE,
                  Flagstaff, Arizona.

November 4, 1897.

    D. M. FRANCIS,
                Flagstaff, Arizona.

November 4, 1897.

    Miss S. L. PHILLIPS,
                  Denver, Colo.

Close of season 1897.

April 25, 1898.

    J. J. LONERGAN,
                Los Angeles, Cal.

April 25, 1898.

    JOHN MARSHALL,
                Flagstaff, Arizona.

April 25, 1898.

    J. M. SIMPSON,
                Flagstaff, Arizona.

Crossed the river below rapids, at foot of Hance's trail, April 27th. Very rough, and high water; 26th, down trail; 27th, across river; 28th, up; 29th, Cameron & Berry mine; 30th, at hotel; May 1st, returned home.

April 26, 1898.

    DENNY BRERETON.

I went to the river with Captain John Hance last Saturday, and I think it enables one to much better appreciate the magnitude and wonders of this great cañon.

May 2, 1898.

    C. H. VEEDER,
                Hartford, Conn.

Snow twelve inches deep.

May 3, 1898.

    EDWIN O. STANARD, Jr.

Went around the rim in a snow-storm. May 4th, started down to the river. Snow and rain all day. Roughest passage Captain Hance ever made (so he says). Weather cleared several times during the day. Trip greatly enjoyed. Would do it again in similar weather, if necessary. Better in a snow-storm than not at all. Time to river, two hours and thirty minutes; back, three hours and thirty minutes.

May 5, 1898.

    H. G. REIST,
                Schenectady, New York.

May 5, 1898.

    CAROLINE CARPENTER,
                Mass.

To take a ride with Capt. Hance,
  On his dead-level trail,
Is sure to fill one's soul with joy,
  Whatever else may fail.

May 10, 1898.

    E. S. MEERS,
                White Hall, Mich.

Self and daughter descended to the river this day on foot, except that my daughter rode up. Captain Hance was very kind and attentive.

May 10, 1898.

    L. A. HEINER,
                Redwood City, Cal.

The Grand Cañon, Nature's crowning work.

May 19, 1898.
   W. R. WEAVER,
            Bradford, Pa.

May 19, 1898.
   Mrs. L. E. HAMSHEAR,
   Mr. L. E. HAMSHEAR,
            Bradford, Pa.

May 19, 1898.
   C. P. COLLINS,
   BURT COLLINS,
            Bradford, Pa.

May 19, 1898.
   WALDA HARDISON,
            Bradford, Pa.

May 19, 1898.
   J. R. LEONARD,
            Beaver, Pa.

May 19, 1898.
   GEO. W. CRAWFORD,
            Emlinton, Pa.

May 19, 1898.
   HARRY HEASLEY,
            Emlinton, Pa.

May 30, 1898.
   Mrs. GEO. P. BOWLER.

May 30, 1898.
   Miss A. HUNT.

May 30, 1898.
   DAVID WILLCOSC.

May 30, 1898.
   VICTOR MORAMETZ.

June 2, 1898.
   JAS. M. HIXON,
            Lacrosse, Wis.

June 4, 1898.
   MAURICE LONGENECKER,
            Cincinnati, Ohio.

June 4, 1898.
   E. R. WEBSTER,
            Cincinnati, Ohio.

June 5, 1898.
   E. BURTON HOLMES,
            Chicago, Ill.

WATERFALL, GRAND CAÑON.

June 5, 1898.
　　OSCAR B. DEPUE,
　　　　　　Chicago, Ill.

June 7, 1898.
　　MARY V. WORSTELL,
　　　　　　New York City, N. Y.

　Drummond, to the contrary, the greatest thing in the world is the Grand Cañon of the Colorado.

June 12, 1898.
　　JAMES N. SUYDAM,
　　　　　　San Francisco, Cal.

June 22, 1898.
　　Mrs. JAMES GAYLER,
　　　　　　Ridgewood, N. J.

June 24, 1898.
　　C. P. WILSON,
　　　　Pastor M. E. Church, Flagstaff.

June 24, 1898.
　　Mrs. W. S. ROBINSON,
　　　　　　Flagstaff, Arizona.

June 24, 1898.
　　ANNETTE P. WARD,
　　　　　　Columbus, Ohio.

July 5, 1898.
　　C. D. STEWART.

　Four of us left hotel at 5:30 A.M., and went to the river and back on foot. We were five hours descending. Coming back, two of us got up before dark; one was brought up on a horse at 9:30, and one stayed all night in the cañon. The moral of this is that one must be a mountaineer in experience and in perfect form for tramping, if he will walk down to the river and back the same day. The heat is intense and overpowering on the lower levels, because the rocks are bare of foliage, and when they become heated by the sun the trail is like a baker's oven. By all means go to the river. The experience alone is worth the trip; but take a horse, or mule even, if you do not take a guide. The trail is as good a mountain trail as is often found, and the Captain's stock are well-selected animals, and are good ones, as one of the four mentioned above.

July 5, 1898.
　　SHURLEY C. WALKER,
　　　　　　San Francisco, Cal.

　I enjoyed the experience immensely, more on account of its success as a pedestrian trip than because I reached the river. Result, fifteen hours' work, one gallon water, gain in muscle, loss in flesh, plenty of experience. Hoping to be indorsed by all the other three companions, I remain,　Yours.

July 6, 1898.
　　EDWARD N. BUTT.

　I have had much experience in mountain-climbing, and German professors also do much good work in that way, but I shall never forget the forlorn appearance of Herr Dr. ——, Professor of Geography, who, when our party were descending to the river to-day, we discovered lying on the ground, in the shade of a tree, at 9 A.M., about an hour down from the rim. He had then been two hours in the great gulf of the Grand Cañon; was utterly exhausted, and had been without food or water for many long, weary hours. Moral. Do not attempt to descend or ascend the Grand Cañon on foot, but take one of Captain Hance's mules.

July 5, 1898.
ROBERT L. STEPHENSON,
San Francisco, Cal.

Our pleasures here have been enhanced by chivalrous, daring, entertaining, and ever-obliging Captain Hance. Hence, it gives us pleasure second only to that of viewing the cañon, to attest to his faithful, careful, and vigilant guidance at all times and to all places.

MARY ASCHERER,
San Francisco, Cal.

ELIZABETH F. BARTLETT,
San Francisco, Cal.

J. SELBY HANNA,
San Francisco, Cal.

GEO. M. SMITH,
Anheuser Wells, Ariz.

EDWARD BUTT,
London, England.

SARAH C. SCOFIELD,
San Antonia, Texas.

EMEUAL D. CALLAGHAN,
W. F. CALLAGHAN,
England.

July 15, 1898.
C. P. HICKS.

July 15, 1898.
J. L. SIMMONS,
Prescott, A. T.

July 30, 1898.
EVA ESTELLA MARTIN.

Our party took in what is called the "rim view" yesterday. No words can in any way describe it. There are hundreds and hundreds of cañons and great ducal palaces put into one great, vast cañon. After all is said the trip is made very much pleasanter by the companionship of Captain Hance. Some one really ought to write a book all about the Captain.

July 30, 1898.
EMMA and GEO. F. HARRINGTON,
Crown King, Ariz.

Had the author of the creation viewed

this majestic scene what wonderful symphonies would have been composed by this Master of Choral Composition. The marvelous work, behold, amazed, comes to one's mind constantly while viewing the Grand Cañon. I shall not attempt to describe the sight, but shall urge my friends to go and see for themselves, and the guidance and companionship of Captain Hance is invaluable. No visitor of the Grand Cañon can afford to make the mistake of failing to appreciate his rugged humor and great kindness of heart.

July 30, 1898.

BELL MARTIN,
Webster,
Westmoreland Co., Pa.

We stood and gazed on the Grand Cañon with feelings of reverence and awe, and involuntarily exclaimed, "How marvelous are Thy works, Oh Lord! In wisdom hast Thou made them all." Our trip around the rim, under the careful guidance of Captain John Hance, was most delightful, but words fail when one attempts to describe it.

July 30, 1898.

FLORA DUNCAN,
Mt. Pleasant, Penn.

Alex and Kitty are the ones. Get Alex for the trip around the rim, Kitty for the trip down in the cañon. The Captain is an excellent guide. The going down in the cañon is easy. I don't think the same about coming out.

July 30, 1898.

EDNA FAY MARTIN,
Prescott, A. T.

The Captain calls me the "Prescott Kid."

July 30, 1898.

GEO. M. SMITH,
Kas. City, Mo.

After seventy days' search, I fail to find words with which to express my thoughts of the Grand Cañon,— of its immensity, its grandeur, and beauty. I cannot believe that man can describe it. Many thanks to the famous Captain John Grand Cañon Hance, for his many kindnesses during my stay.

July 30, 1898.

E. T. HUTCHINS,
Philadelphia, Pa.

Our Captain deserves great credit in being able to build such a wonderful trail.

August 10, 1898.

M. P. FREEMAN,
Tucson, Ariz.

Captain John Hance, old man, you are a "brick" in every sense of the word. Your company has added much to the pleasure of my stay. I shall not forget you.

M. C. HAST AND WIFE.

We made the trip down the cañon in fine shape, due to our good guide and companion, Captain John Hance. Long may he live.

August 12, 1898.
    E. BURTON HOLMES,
                    Chicago, Ill.

August 12, 1898.
    ARTHUR STUDD,
              London, England,
              Chicago, Ill.

August 12, 1898.
    R. N. RIPLEY,
                    Chicago, Ill.

August 12, 1898.
    ORCAR B. DEPUE,
                    Chicago, Ill.

August 12, 1898.
    Mrs. J. M. HENDERSON,
    Miss J. F. HENDERSON,
    CHAS. A. HENDERSON,
    H. H. HENDERSON,
    F. B. HENDERSON,
              Los Angeles, Cal.

August 12, 1898.
    EMMA KERR,
                  Watsonville, Cal.

August 16, 1898.
    RICHARD E. SLOAN,
    Mrs. R. SLOAN,
    Mrs. R. S. STOCKTON,
    RICHARD S. STOCKTON,
    ELEANOR SLOAN,
    RICHARD SLOAN, Jr.,
            All of Prescott, Ariz.

August 16, 1898.
    Miss BELLA CASSIN,
                Watsonville, Cal.

August 16, 1898.
    C. H. CALKVEN,
              Amsterdam, Holland.

August 23, 1898.
    FRANCES O. FISHER,
                  Prescott, Ariz.

August 23, 1898.
    Miss BLANCH FERRINGTON,
                Phoenix, A. T.

August 23, 1898.
    Mrs. J. W. FRANCIS,
    LeNORE FRANCIS,
    FRANK BEAL,
    ALLEN DAVISON,
              All of Flagstaff, A. T.

    THEO. L. SCHULTZ,
    Mrs. THEO. L. SCHULTZ,
              Tempe, A. T.

August 23, 1898.
    Miss FANNIE HICKETHIER,
              Los Angeles, Cal.

August 24, 1898.
    Mrs. JOHN Y. T. SMITH,
              Phoenix, A. T.

August 24, 1898.
    Mrs. T. L. SHULTZ,
              Tempe, Ariz.

August 25, 1898.
    Miss AGNES B. TODD,
              Los Angeles, Cal.

August 26, 1898.
    CHESTER P. DORLAND,
              Los Angeles, Cal.
    Captain John Hance,— a genius, a philosopher, and a poet, the possessor of a fund of information vastly important,— if true. He laughs with the giddy, yarns to the gullible, talks sense to the sedate, and is a most excellent judge of scenery, human nature, and pie. To see the cañon only, and not to see Captain John Hance, is to miss half the show.

August 27, 1898.
    P. MINOR AND WIFE,
              Phoenix, A. T.

August 27, 1898.
    E. T. STIMSON AND WIFE,
              Los Angeles, Cal.

September 5, 1898.
    KATE L. BASSETT,
              Phoenix, A. T.

September 5, 1898.
    Mrs. R. B. BURNS,
              Williams, A. T.

September 5, 1898.
    SAM R. BETTS,
              New York City.

September 5, 1898.
    G. W. PHELCO,
              Tucson, A. T.

September 5, 1898.
   FRED WETZLER.

September 5, 1898.
   JENNIE EDETH GRAY,
            Lyndon, Vermont.

Five days long to be remembered.

September 7, 1898.
   J. K. HARE,
            New York City, N. Y.

Captain Hance's birthday, forty-eight years old. May his years to come be as many as the tales he tells; but this, we are afraid, would prolong his life far into the millennium.

September 7, 1898.
   J. F. FLAGG,
   Miss FLAGG.

September, 7, 1898.
   R. B. WILLIAMSON,
            Los Angeles, Cal.

September 12, 1898.
   ARTHUR R. REYNOLDS,
            Chicago, Ill.

I believe all the Captain's stories to be true, and if any one in the future should doubt, send him to me that I may do battle with him. To Captain John Hance, Grand Cañon of the Colorado.

September 13, 1898.
   JAMES SMITH,
            Flagstaff, Arizona.

It is unfortunate that the words grand, sublime, and awful have been so overworked. These words, which otherwise might have been useful in expressing one's thoughts of the Grand Cañon, John Hance, etc., have so lost their meaning that English fails to express my thoughts. All that I can do is to say that this, the Grand Cañon of the Colorado River, is the grandest sight on earth.

September 15, 1898.
   C. F. GUNTHER,
            Chicago, Ill.

September 19, 1898.
   EDMUND J. BART.

It's a ditch of all the ditches. That's all.

September 19, 1898.
   EDMOND CARLETON,
            New York City, N. Y.

With sincere admiration for Captain John Hance, the faithful custodian of the greatest natural curiosity and most sublime formation in the world.

September 19, 1898.
   Mrs. NORMAN W. CUTTER,
            San Jose, Cal.

ORIGINAL HANCE CABIN, 1885.

September 20, 1898.

WM. BRIDHAM.

See the Grand Cañon, and know Captain Hance, you will never forget them, sure thing.

September 21, 1898.

Mr. and Mr. C. M. BERGSTRES-SER,
New York City, N. Y.

This is Mr. John Hance's book, and no record of a trip through the cañon without reference to Mr. Hance, his company as a guide, is good, to say the least. His knowledge of the cañon is extensive, and his trail has passed into history as one of the most famous in the cañon. His genial nature, and his anecdotes and Indian tales, add much to the pleasure of doing the cañon.

September 21, 1898.

CHAS. H. TOWNSEND.
U. S. Fish Commissioner.

To Captain John Hance, of the Grand Cañon: Good-by; and may it be many a year before you take the trail to the camp from which no one comes back.

September 23, 1898.

JNO. J. VALENTINE.

My Dear Captain Hance: Hoping that the dear Lord may be good to you, and not call for you too soon.

September 23, 1898.

Miss M. J. VALENTINE.

Many good wishes for a long and prosperous life is my wish for you, Captain.

September 23, 1898.

MARY E. PRIDHAM.

Captain Hance, I hope to hear of your finding that fish-hook.

September 23, 1898.

ETHEL VALENTINE.
San Francisco, Cal.

Many appreciations to Captain John Hance for adding greatly to the pleasure of my trip to the Grand Cañon. A comedy without the comedian is not fully enjoyed; the cañon, without Captain Hance, is not complete.

September 23, 1898.

WM. H. ZINN.

The thing I most admire about Captain John Hance is his conscientious truthfulness. I have perfect faith in all of the stories he has told me.

September 26, 1898.

EDWIN A. BECK.

Shall hope some day to return and ride Cape Horn with you, and take one more ride to the river.

September 26, 1898.

EARL C. ANTHONY.

Hope to return again and take some more photographs, with Captain Hance's able assistance.

September 26, 1898.

CHAS. E. ANTHONY.

My trip with you has been glorious, and my only regret is that I did not take the trip to the river with you. Hope to come again some time, Captain, simply for that ride.

October 1, 1898.

R. and E. E. F. SKEEL.

Farewell to the gorge,
And to Captain John Hance,
Whose mendacious inventions outdo all romance.
With his fibs he can charm, with his yarns he enchants;
And as if these great gifts to still further enhance,
With a bolster he is going to learn how to dance.
Oh may we return, by some rare, happy chance,
To this spot, and be welcomed by Captain John Hance.

October 6, 1898.

LOTTIE SHERWOOD,
MAUD SHERWOOD,

Winslow, A. T.

FRANK C. REID.

The Grand Cañon is an expression of God's mightiest thought, and is not transferable into terms of human speech,— one of the things "not possible to be uttered."

ANNETTE P. WARD.

Since seeing that great wonder, the Grand Cañon, I never hear a bit of beautiful, soul-stirring music but that the cañon rises before my inner vision. Listening to the exquisite strains of harmony, I gaze into that indescribable beauty of coloring which enwraps those awful, weird, mysterious depths, and like a soft accompaniment to the music, I hear the sighing of the pines; and the harmony of the music and the harmony of the enchanting beauties of the scene are blended into one perfect whole,— a veritable feast for the memory.

HEAD OF COTTONWOOD CAÑON — ON GRAND VIEW TRAIL.

THE GRAND CAÑON OF THE COLORADO.

What wrought this wonder?
Unique, stupendous, weird and grand!
How came it here — at whose command?
Not Jove with all his bolts of thunder
Could blast and tear these rocks asunder,
And leave them where they stand.

What monster dart,
Or blade, did angry demons wield
To smite earth's breast, is not revealed; —
Nor why they tore the wound apart; —
As if to find her bleeding heart —
So that it never healed.

The thought dismiss.
The fiercest blast — the rudest shock
From Pluto's fiery realm, but mock
The mighty power which fashioned this
Yawning gulf, — this vast abyss: —
These battlements of rock!

Perchance we may
Let sage and hoary Neptune tell
How, by their own erodic spell,
The ocean currents wore away
These rocks, in some far distant day,
And carved these forms so well.

We stand aghast
Upon this brink! nor hear the flow,
By which this desert stream, we know,
Still fights its way — as in the past —
Six thousand feet below.

Here silence reigns,
And here, where science too is mute,
We leave to fools the vain dispute.
We call!—no voice an answer deigns:—
These awful depths but mock our pains:—
Profundus absolute!

C. R. PATTEE.

SCENE IN THE STALACTITE CAVES IN THE GRAND CAÑON.

THE STALACTITE CAVES OF THE GRAND CAÑON.

J. CURTIS WASSON.

Perhaps the destined single attraction of the Grand Cañon is the new Stalactite Caves, lately discovered about 3,000 feet below the rim. The formations within the caves are something wonderful. Passing in through an aperture some eight feet in diameter, a large avenue of limestone leads you on until you are suddenly surprised to find yourself standing in a large rotunda with a great high ceiling, suspended from which are long stalactite formations, some so long in fact that they almost reach the stalagmite formations protruding from the floor beneath.

Winding in and out, up and down, through long cavernous recesses, now through a tunnel leading to greater and longer tunnels, which in turn act as a vestry, making an entrance to other large domes, which, having avenues after avenues leading out to other domes, halls, recesses, avenues, etc., until the feet becoming weary we, candles in hand, sit down upon some snowy formation beneath, and while the candles flicker, as if offering a faint murmur against the impenetrable darkness, which feign would obscure our vision with its itensity, the awful stillness seems to bear down upon all mental activity and bid it relegate all thought to the rear.

But as if in defiance of that awful foreboding which seems to come when the fall of a footstep, the breaking away of a formation, or the sound of a voice finds the sequel in the echo and re-echoing of each cavern, dome, avenue, and pit in that great subterranean cavern where King Phantom may reign supreme with a retinue of fairies, imps, and hobgoblins to go at his bidding,—in defiance of this our mind unconsciously lingers on the uniqueness of the situation.

Our lights having been extinguished, we await the awful stillness which a place thus isolated alone can give,—so intense in fact that the darkness of a Plutonian Shore becomes a veritable lighthouse.

Our heart-beats becoming audible, and the darkness becoming depressing with its intensity, it is with great relief that we again relight our candles, doubling the number.

Looking directly in front some twenty feet, we see towering upward a great massive artificial edifice made by the constant dripping of ages. Bearing as it did such a strong resemblance to another great historic edifice we (as our eyes were first to see this the Second Cave discovered) called it the "Hanging Garden of Babylon."

The fantastic forms, the enormous dimensions, the variegated coloring, from a pure white to a rich creamy hue, the graduated blending of one form, texture, color into another quite different, but none the less beautiful, the soft, velvety-cushioned floor, the disintegrated dust of the ages, the musical tones varying in pitch given off by the stalactite formations as they varied in length,— all these tend to make this — Babylon's Cave — a typical cave, more beautiful than the Mammoth, but whose extent is as yet unknown.

THE HANCE FALLS, GRAND CAÑON.

THE WORLD IS CLEFT.

THE BIGGEST HOLE IN THE GROUND IN EXISTENCE — NATURE PLOWED A GIANT FURROW.

Fitz-Mac Has Been Viewing the Wonders of the Grand Canon of the Colorado, and Tells What He Saw and What Was Too Big for Him to Fully See.

[From the Rocky Mountain News, Denver, Colo.]

Shrive yourself, O gabbling and exclamatory seeker of wonders! Shrive yourselves, O wearied and wearisome trotters of the round and whirling globe! If hither you are coming to bathe your fretted spirits in the red and yellow silences of this abysmal scene, shrive yourselves ere you approach, of all your little vain conceits, of all your petty, gabbling rhetorical formulas of exclamatory ecstasy. They have served you well enough, no doubt, to voice the whole gamut of your delight, surprise, and amazement in the presence of such noble and pleasing wonders as Niagara, Yosemite, Yellowstone, or even the Alps, but such safe and well-authorized exclamations as "Magnificent!" "Grand!" "Sublime!" have only a remote and altogether inadequate relation to the emotions that will be stirred within you by the appalling grandeurs of this stupendous chasm. They do very well for Niagara, or Yosemite, or the Alps, where the emotions you experience though unusual are not unique. But here they do not fit. They do not half go round the girth of your amazement. They are altogether inadequate, and to utter them would be like offering the jacket of a schoolboy to clothe the shoulders of a giant. And if you do utter them, they will sound, even to your own ears, petty and almost meaningless — unless, indeed, you be one of those inexorable egotists whose sturdy self-complacency no emotion can subordinate, in which case, of course, anything you could say would seem to yourself to dignify the occasion and the scene.

But if you be only the amiable, chattering, inquisitive, commonplace globe-trotter and searcher-out of wonders, shrive yourself, I say, of all your little, shallow affectations of delight; of all those petty formulas of rhetorical ecstasy which elsewhere very well conceal the hungry poverty of your feelings, for they would not serve you in this tragic and stupendous presence, but only shame you by their inadequacy.

Pause as you approach, and remove the sandals from your feet, as one who hath sinned goeth up unto the holy places of the Lord seeking absolution. For thou hast sinned, O gushing and exclamatory globe-trotter! thou hast sinned against the majesty and the power of Nature by rashly exclaiming in the presence of great Niagara, "*Ne plus ultra!* this is greatest!"—or in the sublime shades of deep Yosemite by crying out, "There is nothing else so grand!"—or perchance, gazing entranced upon the sky-piercing majesty of the Alps thou hast said conclusively: "This is greater than all besides! here Nature hath done her uttermost!"

But your rash conclusiveness has betrayed you, O shallow chatterer, into denying the power of Nature to surprise, to astonish, to amaze, to thrill, to overawe, to subdue and reduce, to silence your puerile, self-deceiving, exclamatory egotism by the tragic anguish of devastation immeasurable and the bewildering mystery of splendors unique, resistless, and overwhelming here presented. Here you might lose a hundred Yosemites and never be able to find them again. Here a dozen Niagaras would form but details in the stupendous scene. You might scatter the whole mass of the Alps through the 700 miles of this abysmal chasm without filling it up.

It behooves you to come humbly and with bared feet into the presence of a wonder that dwarfs all other wonders of the world — for it is here and not elsewhere that Nature hath done her uttermost; here a world's sublimest tragedy was enacted — is still enacting with all scenes set; the *tableau vivant* of an immortal anguish, a glorified despair; pride and strength laid low and beauty bleeding; the triumph of chaos and devastation; a petrified woe, yet not ghastly and forbidding, strange to say, but fascinating, for this imperial tragedy of Nature is not set amidst ignoble and plebeian scenes, but is draped and curtained with every charm of color, with all the massive and imposing dignity of Pompeiian reds and yellows, with all the imperial magnificence of the Tyrian purple; with all the gorgeous splendors of orange hues and violet that go with a tropical sunset; with all the pensive beguilement of tender amber-greenish lights that belong to the creeping break of dawn — and all these, the massive, the gorgeous, the magnificent, the sensuous, the brilliant, the mellow, the tender, swept and swirled by great Nature's unerring brush into a ravishing, harmonious, chromatic maze that bursts upon the view with an effect as if the skies had opened and all the choirs of heaven had broken into a grand and joyful overture, an allegro through which runs a penetrating minor chord of tragic sadness.

And it is so, somewhat, if you have the impressional delicacy to feel it. Otherwise of course it is not so at all to you. For it is true — or else the sympathy of one sense with another beguiles the reason — that the colors in this ravishing chromatic maze are endued with the magic of melody and odor.

But this is something incommunicable. It is probably not a thing to be insisted upon as a fact. Either you feel it or it is not so — for you.

I met a beautiful girl from Chicago out on "the rim" — locally here they call the verge of the chasm the rim — the other morning before sunrise, who was profoundly affected by it. She was a lovely and sensitive creature, just graduated from a fashionable boarding-school, and she was eating caramels and sobbing like a lost child.

Anybody not quite as stolid and unimpressionable as the ox is pretty sure to have a sobbing spell here, especially if one gets off alone and yields himself up to the stupendous impressions of the scene, the sensation is so unique, so penetrating, so irresistible. It is really something of a pain — a sweet discomfort, a miserable bliss — like being in love, sadly and tearfully in love, with a girl who is going to marry another fellow — like but not the same. The inexorable most always affects us somewhat like that, and the unique beauty of this scene is of the inexorable sort. You may enjoy it, but you cannot possess it. You can add nothing to it by praise, take nothing from it by detraction. It is not the matchless immensity of it, I think, that overcomes you, but that your senses cannot quite encompass and analyze its unique and elusive quality. At first it is more or less appalling, I think, to everybody — but only just at first, as an elephant would be to a little child. Presently, like the child with the elephant, finding it does not crush you, you desire to become familiar with it, to patronize it, to make it feel that your intentions are entirely friendly. And then the elephantine impassiveness of the thing begins to irritate you, and yet to fascinate. Next you know you are in love with it. You want to remain forever; you want to leave at once; you don't know what you want.

It is thus love always begins, thus always proceeds — at least as far as I know anything about it. If you could only quarrel with this stupendous thing, and fling back at its feet all the beautiful things it has given you, then burst into tears and kiss and make up, it would be perfect. But you can't do it, you know. This great thing that frightens you by its appalling immensity, that enthralls you by the magic of its matchless beauty, that bewilders and mystifies your senses by the vague, odoriferous minor tones of its melodious purples, and by the vast, echoless silences of its Pompeiian reds and yellows, is inexorable to your puny emotions. That is what irritates you, what makes you sob unconsciously as you gaze off into the illimitable chromatic maze.

Hither, to this point, long ago came Thomas Moran, the painter, and painted for the people of the United States that great scene which hangs in the capitol, and which, no doubt, has damaged his reputation with many people who regard it as a hysterical exaggeration, a sort of beautiful chromatic nightmare.

But Moran's reputation will be utterly ruined with such people

COCONINO CYCLE CLUB — LEAVING THE GRAND CAÑON, 1897.

when they see the grand chasm for themselves, and learn what broad concessions he made to the public incredulity regarding the scene.

But for a truth the finest effects here are incommunicable by brush or pen. They give themselves up only to the personal presence, and no painter nor writer can do more than suggest what they are by presenting something which they are a little like. You cannot paint a silence, nor a sound, nor an odor, nor an emotion, nor a sob. If you are skillful, you may suggest them to the imagination by some symbol understood, and Moran's fine picture does this admirably. It gives one sublime glimpse of those abysmal depths, one irresistible suggestion of those vast and sublime silences, one momentary flash of that marvelous scheme of color suggesting melody and fragrance—but only suggesting. Yet that is all which human skill can do with brush or pen. There are not colors for the brush, there are not symbols for the pen to convey the full impression of the immensity of the scene, its innumerable and measureless grandeurs. The scene in its stupendous ensemble is too vast for art. It is indeed almost too much for human nature. You cannot behold it for the first time without a gasp, however *blasé* your spirits may have become by globe-trotting, because the spectacle is unique, and the impression is therefore unique too.

There is a sublime pathos in it all which no art I think can touch—or scarcely touch, for on reflection, I am not sure but Moran's noble picture does vaguely suggest it. It is this that presses the unconscious sob from your breast, that draws the pensive tears to your eyes, you know not why, as you gaze—that is, if you happen to be gazing alone. It is as if you dreamed that God had died, and this deep chasm were the gorgeous and sublime sepulchre in which He was to be laid—but of course if you are a natural insensate or a busy, gabbling, inquisitive, wearisome wonder-seeker, shallow of heart and shallow of head, you will be troubled by none of that vague, unique anguish about the death of God, or that equally vague and equally unique joy about the discovery of melody and fragrance in those massive and gorgeous colors that give enchantment to the scene. You are altogether too practical and conclusive a being to think of getting any spiritual growth from the innumerable and incommunicable sublimities of this place. All that you want is facts — facts and statistics of measurement to write down in that detestable note-book you are carrying around in your hand. You have no time for vague and nebulous impressions about fragrant and melodious colors swathing the sepulchre of God. You are not rendered blissfully miserable by the strange emotions which the splendors and the immensity of the spectacle arouse within you. You don't want any vague, nebulous, incommunicable, soul-broadening sentimentality in yours — not if you know yourself. What you want is something to gabble about after you leave — measurements, facts, and figures.

Do I know how many thousand feet it is down to the bottom of the chasm where we catch, here and there, a glimpse of a little ribbon of water? Do I think it is really nearly 7,000 feet in the perpendicular and about three miles in the slant — five by the trail? Is the trail safe? Is it dangerous? Does it really take two days to go down and back? Can it be possible? Do I think that it is really and truly thirteen miles across to the opposite rim of the chasm? Why it looks as if one might call to a person over there. Can it be possible that this chasm is 700 miles long? Do I believe it? Is n't it incredible that we can be standing here on this rim in the very center of the whole geological series of the earth's crust, with that yawning abyss reaching more than a mile deeper, and the river running in the archean granite? How can they know that the geological horizon in which we are standing here on this rim is the upper carboniferous? By this cherty limestone? Is cherty spelled c-h-u-r-t-y or c-h-i-r? Do I believe the Government really paid Moran $18,000 for a picture?

Sir, or madam, whichever your sex may be, you are no doubt a perfectly respectable and worthy person, but to me, at this time and in this place, you are, with your gabbling, inquisitive tongue and your note-book, an insufferable bore. Pray address your questions to somebody interested in the mensurations and the geology of this overwhelming spectacle. I am only concerned with the impressions it makes upon my senses, and I don't care a —— whether it is 7,000 feet or 7,000 miles down to the bottom of the chasm. To me it is just as far as it seems, and I don't care what the figures are. It is the deepest, the most stupendous, the most appalling, the most mystically beautiful, the most sublimely pathetic — in a word, the most moving and irresistible tragedy I have ever beheld or ever expect to, and I wish you would leave me to enjoy my own impressions. As you are unable to share them, I beg that you will be so good as not to interrupt them with questions in mensuration and kindergarten geology. I don't know whether cherty is spelled with u or i or an ox-yoke, and I don't care a ——. All that you ask, and a thousand times more, you will find authoritatively stated in the reports of several scientific surveys made by the Government and printed as public documents.

They will be found in any public library worthy of the name in the United States. Ask the librarian to let you see the Report on the Expedition of Lieutenant Whipple, in 1853-4; the Expedition of Lieutenant Ives, in 1858; that of Major Powell, about 1868; that by Lieutenant Wheeler, published in 1875, vol. III, and whatever else has followed. If you have not easy access to a large public library, send to "The Bureau of Scientific Surveys, Washington," (this is not the exact title, but it will do,) and ask for a catalogue of the publications bearing on the Grand Cañon of the Colorado. From this you can select what you want, and perhaps obtain it free through your Member of Congress; if not, the cost is but a trifle.

Major Powell's book is the thing you should get.

The railroad does not come within sixty-five miles of the Grand Cañon. You leave the cars at Flagstaff, Arizona, and come out by the daily stage. It is an easy and delightful ride of ten or eleven hours, most of the way through the beautiful, park-like Coconino pine forest and "The National Grand Cañon Reserve," which contains about 2,000,000 acres. The road lies along the base of the beautiful San Francisco Mountains, and you are whirled along at breezy speed, in an easy coach, behind a champing four-in-hand team, through a charming succession of sylvan scenes, in a crisp and bracing atmosphere that comes to your lungs laden with homely odor of pine and the bewitching fragrance of wild flowers. The horses are changed four times on the way and so are always fresh, and there is none of the old, dusty, thumping stage-coach sensation of dragging along.

Come to see it. There is no hardship in the journey. You must not conclude that because it is in Arizona it will be found hot. The altitude prevents. All the way from Flagstaff " to the rim " it is about 7,000 feet.

Come and see it. The trip will be a grand episode in your life. The matchless spectacle will become a noble and deathless memory.

Come and behold the marvelous vision where silence has dimension and color; where color has melody and fragrance.

Come and dream of the gorgeous and appalling sepulchre of God and then you will realize how inadequately I have, in this hasty sketch, suggested to your imagination its stupendous glories and its sublime pathos. FITZ-MAC.

HOTEL AND TENTS AT THE GRAND CAÑON.

THE GRAND CAÑON CAVERN.

[From the Coconino Sun, Flagstaff, Arizona.]

To a cook named Joseph Gildner, employed in the mining camp of Messrs. Cameron & Berry in the Grand Cañon of the Colorado near Flagstaff, Arizona, belongs the honor of discovering what savants had looked for in vain, although they had every reason to presume that what they sought was in existence, and what geologists have long desired to find, in the hope that some further light might be thrown upon some matters connected with the geological formation of the Grand Cañon, which hitherto could only be conjectured. It has long been contended that if caves could only be discovered some more definite information could be gleaned of the many thousands of feet of strata which it is claimed by geologists have been swept away by erosion from the surface of this platform. Several of the caves have lately been discovered, but only one so far has been partially explored, and that is the one located by the man Gildner.

Standing on Clear Creek Cañon, a mile below the plateau on which the camp and mines are situated, and looking up at the entrance to this cave, one is filled with vague horror and amazement at the mere thought of any one venturing to climb along the precipitous face of the mountain to explore its depths. Even with the aid of a powerful glass it does not seem possible that a chamois or mountain goat could find a foothold there. How the man ever got there in the first instance without a rope or any other assistance and escaped falling down and being dashed to pieces at the base of the rock, a precipitous descent of over 1,000 feet, is a mystery. But certain it is he got there and found two entrances to the cave, through one of which he was barely able to drag his body, but the vision he there beheld in the dim, imperfect light made him quickly withdraw and acquaint the manager and active partner of the mine, Mr. P. D. Berry, with his discovery.

The cliff in which this cave was discovered rises almost abruptly from the plateau on which the camp is situated, and frowns down menacingly on the cañon below. It is truly a very forbidding object, composed of a dirty reddish limestone formation, and seems to warn the venturesome that death awaits him who would pry too closely into the secrets that Nature has so closely guarded in her impenetrable bosom. But such considerations have but little weight with the men who establish the frontier settlements, and next morning Mr. Berry had a gang of men employed digging a trail from the summit of the plateau to the mouth of the cave. The work was arduous, but the persistent labor of the men was amply rewarded, and now they have got a trail that any one can walk along without danger, a splendid platform at the mouth of the cave about six feet wide, and the entrance has been enlarged until a man can almost walk into it erect.

To describe it as a cave is not literally correct. It is rather an intricate series of caves branching out one from the other, and extending in every direction under the mountains. The first cave or compartment is fully 300 feet long and of varying height, extending from about ten feet in some places to eighty or ninety feet in others, and the view presented to the beholder is almost sufficient to take one's breath away. Pendent from the ceiling and the sides of the cave are the most beautiful formations of stalactite, and the reflection from these as the light of candles or torches is thrown on them is dazzling in its brilliancy. But while the glance is momentarily riveted on the scene here exposed to view, attention is almost insensibly drawn to the floor beneath. There a view is presented that beggars description. At first glance it would seem as if the bottom of the Indian Ocean had been suddenly transplanted for the benefit of the visitors to this cave. Mountain after mountain of coral, pink and white, appear in rapid succession, while sea anemones of every conceivable hue and color seem to float around in endless variety. There are parterres and rows of flowers arranged in such order that it would put any landscape painter to the blush, while the bowers and grottoes that abound might have served as a resting-place for Queen Mab and her fairy satellites.

The second cave is of about the same dimensions as the first, but much higher, and the columns of stalactite are very much larger and more diversified in shape. Here large pieces of stalactite have fallen from the roof and sides of the cave, pressed down by the superincumbent weight, and been shattered to atoms on the floor below, while vast sheets hang from the walls with scarcely any perceptible support, revealing almost every form of animate or inanimate nature, grotesque at times, 't is true, but always with a sufficiently strong resemblance. Here may be found the jaws of leviathan sharks, the serrated rows of teeth looking as ugly as if the monster were springing from the deep to tear down its victim who was being hoisted on board a vessel; there the deadly swordfish, with its cruel, sharp weapon, ever in readiness for attack or defense; while in the most inconceivable places may be found saws of every description, from the tiniest to the big cross-cut.

But the most wonderful sight of all is what is called the "White Cave." Shortly after entering, the visitor is confronted with a lion rampant on a pedestal about eighteen inches long. The figure stands about a foot high and is as nearly perfect in detail as anything that ever left the sculptor's or molder's hands. A few feet from there stands a Burmese pagoda which, when a candle is placed in rear of it, seems to be lighted up as if for service, while the sacred elephant stands out in bold relief in dazzling whiteness, a piece of crystallized lime forming the eye which, with the glare of the candle upon it, seems to flash out luridly and angrily at having been disturbed after ages of repose.

It would be impossible to describe the various compartments the writer went through in a journey of about four hours. Many of them are of such enormous height that the flare of the candles or torches serves to reveal nothing but impenetrable blackness up above, while the sides in all cases are lined with the most fantastic and grotesque shapes. In one place is to be found a bay window, the curtains and window blinds arranged in the most artistic manner, while everywhere you can select your own chime of bells and discourse sweet music with cymbals thrown in.

A peculiar feature about this cave is, that whereas most of the stalactite is formed by white limestone, there is none of that substance now forming the rock, the upper strata being composed of the red limestone, and it will be a question for geologists to determine what period of time has elapsed since this stalactite, whiter than alabaster, was formed. Moreover, everything in the cave at the present time is as dry as tinder, and it would seem as if centuries had elapsed since any water percolated through. A bathroom there is of enormous dimensions, but no trace of water, nor is there any evidence of animal life beyond the nests made by some rats.

The cave varies from about ten feet high at the entrance to where you cannot see the top. Its width is from sixty to seventy feet, but its length has not yet been determined on, and it is simply a matter of conjecture as to where it leads. About 100 feet from the entrance the visitor is confronted with a regular forest of trees from eight to ten feet in height, the branches and leaves being almost as perfect as in a natural forest. And yet these are all formed of stalagmite of dazzling whiteness.

The cave also abounds in grotesque forms pendant from the roof and sides, and any one visiting the Grand Cañon of the Colorado will miss one of the principal attractions if they omit to see them.

GOING TO THE GRAND CAÑON.

AN ENTHUSIASTIC DESCRIPTION.

BY G. WHARTON JAMES, PASADENA, CAL.

The Grand Cañon! God's stupendous masterpiece on earth! A mountain chain turned upside down and thrust into the world's crust, with all its ravines, crests, gorges, ridges, detached peaks and forests, and at the lowest point of the V, made the bed of an immense river. A chaos of color such as no mountain range on earth ever resembled, for, while there are forests, there are hundreds of square miles of bare, barren, solid rock in all the colors, shades and tints of the rainbow, a striking red being the dominant note in this novel harmony of colors. A wilderness of architectural forms such as no other wilderness affords, or dream of earth's paltry builders ever conceived, for here are suggestions for new styles of architecture when Assyrian, Egyptian, Hindoo, Greek, Roman, Tartarian, Gothic, Florentine, Elizabethan, and more modern styles are relegated to the lumber-piles of the ages. Towers, domes, obelisks, palaces, cathedrals, castles innumerable, stupendous in size, grand and majestic in *ensemble*, harmonious in proportion, novel in architecture. With cunning skill the chisels of the ages, the gnawing forces of Nature, have molded and shaped the slowly-yielding rock to suit the mind of the Master Architect, and man, astounded, bewildered, delighted, gazes at the results in entrancement.

Reached from Flagstaff and other points on the great transcontinental line of the Santa Fe Railway, that traveler affords himself a scenic banquet, incomparable and unique, who visits this unequaled "Water-way of the Gods." According to the conceptions of the localized aborigines, this vast chasm was made by their most powerful gods, and to prevent weak, puny, curious man from following them to the abodes of deity, they turned the vast stream of the Colorado River into its depths. But "in the days when the world will be aged" the course of the stream will be diverted, and the gods will come again to earth. And, slightly to the left of Grand View Point, at the head of the Grand View trail, reached from Flagstaff, three-fourths of the way across the cañon can be seen the giant, rocky gateway through which the new-coming gods will make their descent.

Directly across is the vast wall of the great Kaibab plateau, one of the highest portions of the whole rim of the cañon. Slightly to the right, the most imposing of all the towers of this gloriously carved region is one named "Powell's Temple," dedicated to that indefatigable and daring explorer, Major J. W. Powell, formerly director of the United States Geological Survey and the Bureau of Ethnology, and to whose endeavors the exploration of the long and dangerous depths of the cañons of the Colorado was due.

On the south side of the cañon are the Three Castles, on a tilting stratum of rock, and a little beyond is "Ayer's Peak," so named from Mrs. E. E. Ayer, of Chicago, the first white woman who is known to have made the descent to the river at this point.

Several miles to the east, still on the south side, its summit crowned and shaded by a portion of the vast Coconino Forest, is Moran's Point, on which the great artist made his noted painting of the cañon, and, a few miles beyond, is Bissel's Point, from which an extended view is had of the sculptured forms made by the influx of the Little Colorado River, and the open space in the cañon through which the *Colorado Grande* winds its tortuous way towards the sea. Across from Bissel's Point is Cape Final, the last great cape of the Kaibab plateau.

It is from just above this point the real *Grand* Cañon begins. While Marble, Glen, and a score of other cañons higher up the river are stupendous, marvelous, grand, it is only when the river reaches the primeval rock, the granite, of which the foundations of the world are formed, that the sublime depths of this unique waterway are disclosed. For a distance of some two hundred and seventeen miles the river rages and dashes and roars, pouring its tremendous flood headlong to the passage it has cut through the sandy deserts of Eastern California, and this two hundred and seventeen miles only is known distinctively as *The* Grand Cañon. No other cañon in the world should be known by that name, no matter how qualified. Just as it seems irreverent to use the name of the Deity to designate false gods, so is it to use the name of this solitary piece of divinely wrought grandeur for any inferior work.

For over a decade I have been closely studying it, wandering along its rim for hundreds of miles, exploring its side cañons in every direction, and seeking to penetrate to the secrets of its lowest depths. Months and months of familiar study have not lessened its attractions, nor lowered the profound feelings of awe with which it has always impressed me. I return to it constantly as a lover to his mistress, a student to his books, a chemist to the mysteries he would solve, a prospector to the gold he would discover, and ever and always do I find in it new treasures of sublime grandeur, new glories of stupendous carving, new entrancements of gorgeous coloring, all declaring in their own unmistakable language,—

"The hand that made us is Divine."

SCENE ON THE HANCE TRIAL, GRAND CAÑON.

THE GRAND CAÑON.

[From the Coconino Sun, Flagstaff, Arizona.]

The Grand Cañon is the most wonderful geological and spectacular phenomenon known to mankind. It was no exaggeration to call it the sublimest of gorges, the Titan of chasms. There is but one Grand Cañon, and nowhere on earth can its like be found. Language is too faint and weak to convey any adequate idea of the sublimity and grandeur of this most awe-inspiring of Nature's wondrous works. It must be seen to be appreciated, and even then humanity stands aghast, oppressed with an indefinable sense of terror, while at the same time all the senses are charmed with the indescribable beauties that are opened up to the vision. An eminent writer in describing it defined it as "An inferno, swathed in soft celestial fires; a whole chaotic under-world, just emptied of primeval floods and waiting for a new creative world; a boding, terrible thing, unflinchingly real, yet spectral as a dream, eluding all sense of perspective or dimension; outstretching the faculty of measurement, overlapping the confines of definite apprehension."

This stupendous panorama is situated wholly in the northern part of Arizona. Correctly speaking, it is not a cañon, but rather an intricate system of cañons, all subordinate to the river channel, and forming a whole that is fully one thousand square miles in extent.

GRAND CAÑON STAGES AT FLAGSTAFF DEPOT, WITH EXCURSION PARTY ABOUT TO DEPART FOR GRAND CAÑON.

HOW TO GET THERE.

To those to whom the Grand Cañon of the Colorado is a terra incognito a few words may not be amiss as to how to get there. Starting from any point where the Santa Fe railroad has either a direct line of communication, Albuquerque, N. M., is easily reached, and from thence on to Flagstaff, Ariz., the traveler is carried on through some of the most beautiful and diversified scenery of the Rockies. Arriving at Flagstaff a stagecoach is taken to the Grand Cañon. Then the drive is sixty-five miles long, which is easily accomplished in ten hours, there being four relays of horses for the journey, so that the animals are always fresh, and the road being a solid mountain road free from any obstructions, jars and jolts are almost unknown. The course is along what is perhaps the most beautiful scenery in Arizona or elsewhere. For the first twenty miles it lies through a beautiful forest of pine trees, dotted here and there with parks, circling the base of the far-famed San Francisco Mountains, past the pre-historic cave dwellings and away out into the open prairie, relieved by tracts of scrub cedar and pinyon trees, the home of the prairie-dog and antelope. An excellent lunch can be procured at Cedar Ranch, thirty-four miles from Flagstaff, and thence once more away across the prairie through Cottontail Cañon, where geologists can find much to interest them, one side of the cañon, which is only about fifty feet wide, being composed of limestone formation while the opposite side is malapai. Then bounding over the prairie again until Moqui is reached, and a few miles further when the road again lies through the lordly Coconino forest interspersed with sylvan glades and fragrant meadows for about twelve miles.

The caves, which now form one of the principal of the many attractions of the Grand Cañon, can only be reached by the Cameron or Grand View trail.

G. K. Woods,
General Manager Grand Cañon Stage Line.

FOR any further information in regard to the Grand Canon of the Colorado River in Arizona, or this volume, address,

G. K. WOODS,

General Manager Grand Canon Stage Line

Flagstaff, Arizona Ter.

www.ingramcontent.com/pod-product-compliance
Lightning Source LLC
Chambersburg PA
CBHW030245170426
43202CB00009B/634